Folens

Music Works

A complete resource pack for primary music

Carol Donaldson   Carmel McCourt

Acknowledgements

Thanks to Charlie Norman for performing the rap on 'Follow your Heart'.

United Kingdom: Folens Publishers, Apex Business Centre, Boscombe Road, Dunstable, LU5 4RL. Email: folens@folens.com

Ireland: Folens Publishers, Greenhills Road, Tallaght, Dublin 24. Email: info@folens.ie

Poland: JUKA, ul. Renesansowa 38, Warsaw 01-905

Editor: Sara Peacock
Layout artist: Ken Vail Graphic Design, Cambridge
Illustrations: Celia Hart
Cover design: Ken Vail Graphic Design, Cambridge

First published 2006 by Folens Limited.

British Library Cataloguing in Publication Data. A catalogue record for this publication is available from the British Library.

ISBN 1-84303-862-5

Contents

Introduction 4

Self advocacy 5

Lesson 1	The song: 'Follow your Heart'	**5**
Lesson 2	The rhythm	**8**
Lesson 3	Singing techniques	**11**
Lesson 4	The rap	**14**
Lesson 5	Moods and feelings	**17**
Lesson 6	The performance	**20**
Song sheet	Follow your Heart	**23**

Differences and inclusion 24

Lesson 1	The song: 'Family Tree'	**24**
Lesson 2	The rhythm	**27**
Lesson 3	Singing techniques	**30**
Lesson 4	The rap	**33**
Lesson 5	Moods and feelings	**36**
Lesson 6	The performance	**39**
Song sheet	Family Tree	**42**

World poverty 43

Lesson 1	The song 'This Friend of Mine'	**43**
Lesson 2	The rhythm	**46**
Lesson 3	Singing techniques	**49**
Lesson 4	The rap	**52**
Lesson 5	Moods and feelings	**55**
Lesson 6	The performance	**58**
Song sheet	This Friend of Mine	**61**

Notes for song 62

Activities 65

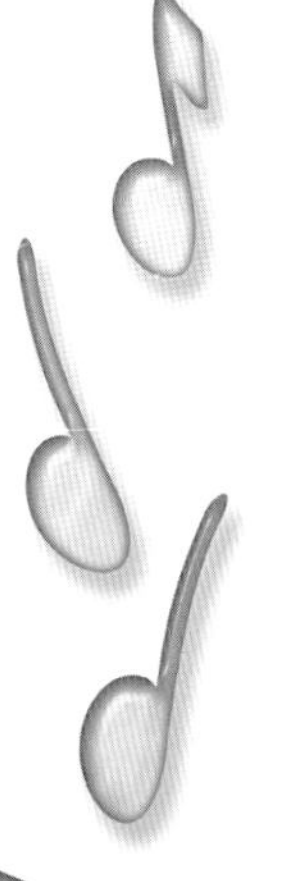

Music Works
Creative Approach to Music in Education

Dear Teacher,
We hope you find this music resource pack helpful and easy to use. The main idea behind this pack is for your lesson-planning to be done for you to enable you to relax. No special musical ability or aptitude is required!

What does *Music Works* do?

Music Works provides three sections for every age group. Within each pack are different themes, for example, for Years 5 and 6, Self advocacy, Differences and inclusion, and World poverty.

Each individual pack contains six 40-minute lesson plans (along with a CD), all working towards the end performance of a specially composed and themed song. The emphasis is on learning through singing, but percussion and rap is also used and, along the way, many music curriculum requirements for Key Stages 1 and 2 will be met.

You are led through each step simply, using the CD tracks to guide you through the song, vocal exercises, rhythm and pulse exercises (all of which are very easy to follow).

Each pack may also be used cross-curriculum with English.

What's different about *Music Works*? The 'WOW' Factor!

This pack has an original contemporary 'pop' song, written especially for *Music Works*. This means the children are more likely to want to engage with it as they will like the sound of it!

Each song has space for a rap in it. Part of this is already written and part of it needs to be written by the class. This seems to work especially well with some of the boys – they identify with rap more easily than some other forms of music and think it's 'cool' to join in with! It encourages them to express themselves and give ideas.

The children also feel the song becomes theirs and is part of their genre – not the teacher's.

How to get the best out of *Music Works*

Read through the lesson plan and get comfortable with starting and stopping your CD player so you don't spend time during the lesson trying to figure out how it works. All machines are slightly different and can thwart the best of us! Make sure you have a good CD player that has sufficient volume.

The feeling that the children 'own' the song rather than the teacher is key to the success and enjoyment of *Music Works* and should be encouraged. (For example, I might say, 'Well, you could do that rap movement with your hands', which I imitate badly and say, 'Oh I can't do it, I'm too old, you show me.' I let them laugh at my pitiful attempts to try to move and rap and they will try to show me and the other children how to do it.)

Children with differing abilities

Children who may not engage in other subjects well can be very musical and the difference between learners is far less obvious.

Ensure that less able children make a big contribution to the rap section. A sense of ownership starts to develop and the resultant building in their confidence is very rewarding.

Note from the authors:
We hope these lessons will be useful to you as a teacher and make learning about music fun for the children. Don't hesitate to let us know how things work or don't work for you so we can update our design and provide you with further resources for the future.

Self advocacy

Lesson 1 The song: 'Follow your Heart'

Music objective

Introducing the song and learning parts of it.

Learning activity

- Vocal warm-up (QCA units 15:1–15:6).
- Building on vocal techniques and building confidence in singing (QCA units 15:1–6).
- Following and learning the verses and choruses in the new song (QCA units 15:7–8).

QCA learning objectives

Unit 15 Ongoing skills

'This unit highlights the musical skills that require regular practice and ongoing development throughout the key stage.'
'Singing songs with control and using the voice expressively.'
Children should learn:

- Section 1 – about breathing, dynamics and accuracy of pitch.
- Section 2 – how to improve tone production and use diction and other vocal techniques, e.g. legato and staccato.
- Section 3 – about pulse, rhythm and metre.
- Section 4 – about phrase and other musical structures.
- Section 5 – to extend their control and understanding of pitch.
- Section 6 – how to make expressive use of elements and techniques and develop their performances.

'Listening, memory and movement.'
Children should learn:

- Section 7 – to listen with sustained concentration; to remember longer pieces of music; about metre.
- Section 8 – to respond physically to music with understanding of musical features.

Scottish attainment targets

Using materials, techniques, skills and media (voice)

- Level C – Sing together confidently in unison with some awareness of dynamics.
- Level B – Show a greater ability to sing in tune with others; fit words to the melody where this is obvious.

Evaluating and appreciating

- Level C – Demonstrate aural retention through playing phrases from familiar tunes by ear; give opinions of own music making and that of others.

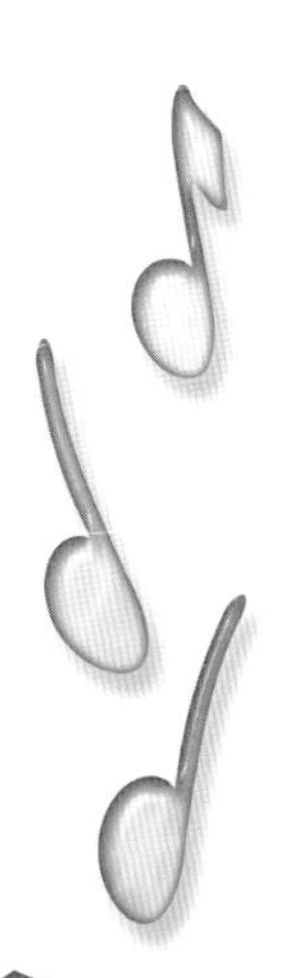

The song: 'Follow your Heart'

1. Play TRACK 1 on the CD – 'Follow your Heart'.

2. Listen again – pointing out the arrangement: the opening chorus, straight into the rap, followed by a middle and finally ending with the chorus: chorus, raps, middle, chorus, chorus out.

3. Carry out a vocal warm-up (for only five minutes or so). This should be a good fun time.
   - Ask the children to form a circle and relax.
   - Tell them to let out a big sigh, then repeat but this time, on the count of three, to hold on to the last note in the sigh. As they sigh, have the children droop to the ground as they finish sighing. Last one standing gets a point!
   - Standing in the circle, ask the children to make circular movements with their arms bent, elbows making circles away from the chest, opening the upper chest and stretching the muscles gently.
   - Next, to get the chest voice going, tell the children to stamp forward after the count of three and shout 'ha', pulling back their elbows as they stamp, then repeating with different vowel sounds: 1, 2, 3, 'HA'; 1, 2, 3, 'HO'; 1, 2, 3, 'HEE'. Now string it together: 1, 2, 3, 'HA', 2, 3, 'HO', 2, 3, 'HEE', 2, 3 and so on. They should do this six times or so.

4. Sing along with TRACK 4 on the CD and learn the chorus with the children.

5. Ask the children to listen out for other voices on the CD and identify what they are doing. Once they have identified that the other voices are singing a harmony, challenge them to see if they can pick out some of the harmony notes that are being sung.

6. Listen to TRACK 5 on the CD, which has the harmony note being sung separately. Choose some of the children to sing along to this. Now listen to the two notes sung together to create a two-part harmony. Sing along to this again, with the children you have chosen singing the harmony and the rest of the class singing the tune, to create the two-part harmony. When the children can sing this section confidently, try it in the context of the song as a whole.

The song: 'Follow your Heart'

7 Listen to TRACK 6 on the CD, encouraging the children to learn the verse.

8 Next, listen to TRACK 7 to enable the children to learn the middle section. They could work in small groups to test each other.

9 Finally, listen to the bridge and rap on TRACK 13 but don't worry about learning this today. Allow anyone who knows how to move to the rap to show the rest of the class, and you, how to move to the beat.

Chill out time!

Have the children sit down at their desks. Each child should lay their head on their arms with eyes closed, breathing slowly through their nose. There should be total silence. Ask them to think about their hobbies, what they like to do in their spare time, their favourite subject at school and whether their hobby or favourite subject could be turned into a job. After two minutes, ask them to open their eyes and sit up, and lead them into sharing their ideas with the rest of the class.

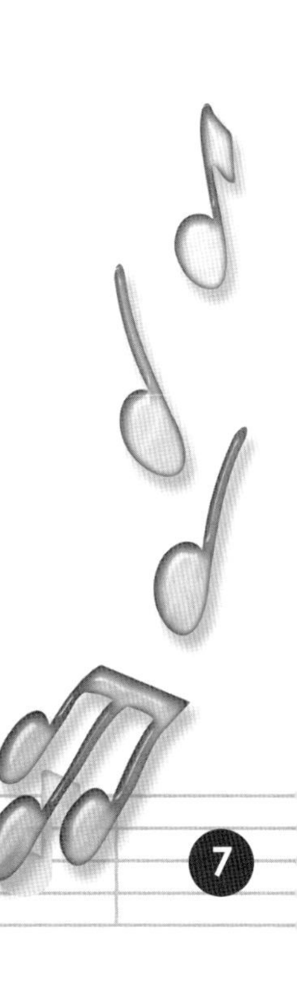

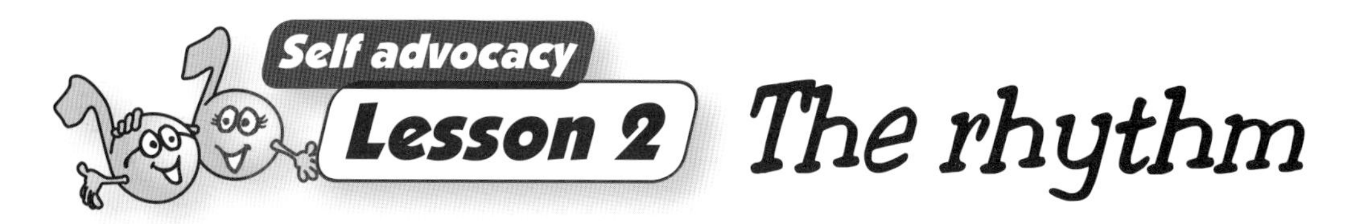

The rhythm

Note – You will be using the percussion trolley for this lesson.

Music objective

Becoming aware of structure, and confidently playing pulse and rhythm parts.

Learning activity

- Playing percussion (rhythm and pulse) (QCA units 16:1–4).
- Remembering the chorus, verse and middle section of the song (QCA unit 15:7).
- Recapping basic techniques for building confidence in singing (QCA unit 15:1).

QCA learning objectives

Unit 15 Ongoing skills

'This unit highlights the musical skills that require regular practice and ongoing development throughout the key stage.'

'Singing songs with control and using the voice expressively.'

- Section 1 – Children should learn about breathing, dynamics and accuracy of pitch.

'Listening, memory and movement.'

- Section 7– Children should learn to listen with sustained concentration; to remember longer pieces of music; about metre.

Unit 16 Cyclic patterns – Exploring rhythm and pulse

'This unit develops pupils' ability to perform rhythmic patterns confidently and with a strong sense of pulse.'

'How does some music use cyclic patterns?'

- Section 1 – Children should learn about cyclic patterns.

'How can different sounds be used rhythmically?'

Children should learn:

- Section 2 – that percussion instruments can produce a wide range of sound.
- Section 3 – how different patterns can fit together.
- Section 4 – about particular cyclic patterns.

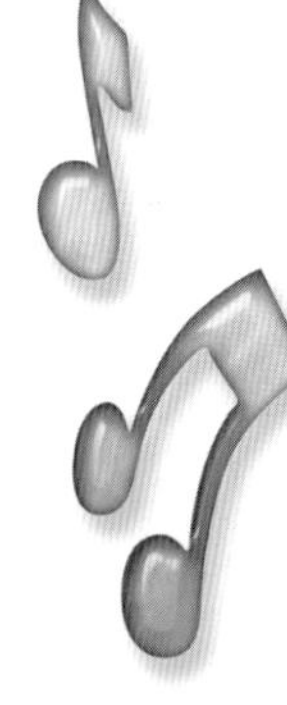

Scottish attainment targets

Using materials, techniques, skills and media (instruments)

- Level B – Play simple rhythmic patterns showing some control over speed and volume.
- Level C – Display two-handed co-ordination in playing straightforward melodies and rhythms.
- Level C – Play confidently on a range of instruments.

Expressing feelings, ideas, thought and solutions

- Level C – Create sound pictures, displaying some imagination with awareness of structure

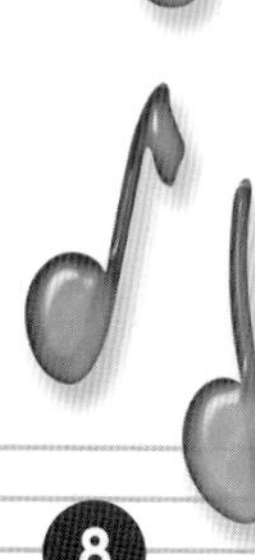

Lesson 2 The rhythm

1. Play TRACK 1 on the CD. Sing along gently with the choruses and middle section.

2. Listen to TRACK 8, which plays the pulse of the song. Clap along with it and count 1, 2, 3 and 4. Ask the children to listen to how this is a steady regular beat – giving us the tempo or speed of the music.

3. Listen to the rhythm on TRACK 9. Point out to the children that it's different to the pulse and the beats are not evenly spaced as before, and encourage them to hear how it fits in well with the pulse. Invite them to suggest another rhythm that would also fit. This rhythm starts on the second beat of the bar (the off-beat), not the first.

4. Split the class in half and have one section clap the pulse and the other section clap the rhythm.

5. Hand out percussion instruments and ask the children with tambourines to play the pulse and those with woodblocks to play the rhythm.

6. Now play along to TRACK 1 with percussion in two parts.

7. Lead a vocal warm-up with the class, but concentrate just on the 'sirens' warm-up. Have the children stand in a circle with their hands resting lightly on their head, and tell them to imitate the sound of a fire engine or a police siren. Remind them that as the sound gets higher, the mouth should get wider, and encourage them to feel the 'buzzing' sensation coming from the top of the head. Ask the children to let their 'siren' sound higher and higher.

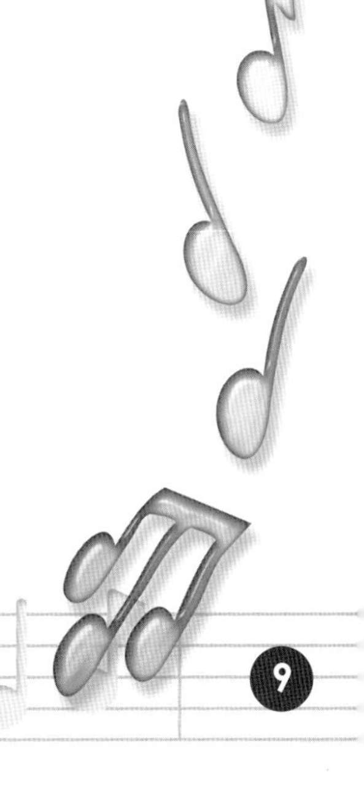

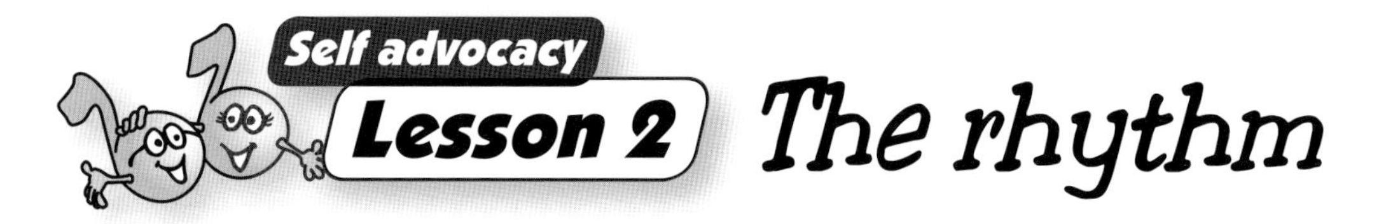

The rhythm

8 Now sing along with the song on TRACK 1 of the CD to refresh everyone's memory. Don't be afraid to sing gently at first – it's more important to make sure the voices are clear and the words are sung with heartfelt expression.

9 Sing through the song again, but this time add the percussion during the rap section.

10 Perform the song using the backing track on TRACK 2, and see how far the children can get without making a mistake.

11 Ask if any of the children would like to sing a verse, a chorus or even try a rap on their own (or in pairs or groups of three). Boys should be encouraged to try at least the rap. Remember to clap the little groups, reminding the class they are all there to support each other.

Chill out time!

Have the children lie down on the floor, close their eyes, and relax in complete silence. After a minute ask them to think about who they would most like to be when they grow up, and who their heroes are and what they do: footballer, singer, actor, teacher, dancer, or scientist perhaps? After a short while ask the children to sit up and to volunteer to share their ideas with the rest of the class. After a short while, tell the children to open their eyes and sit up, then go round the class asking each pupil to name their hero.

Lesson 3 Singing techniques

Music objective

Improve vocal quality and learn the rap section of the song.

Learning activity

- Full vocal warm-up and stretching voice further (QCA unit 15:1).
- Recapping verses and choruses (QCA unit 15:7).
- Learning rap section (QCA unit 15:8).

QCA learning objectives

Unit 15 Ongoing skills

'This unit highlights the musical skills that require regular practice and ongoing development throughout the key stage.'

'Singing songs with control and using the voice expressively.'

- Section 1 – Children should learn about breathing, dynamics and accuracy of pitch.

'Listening, memory and movement.'

Children should learn:

- Section 7 – to listen with sustained concentration; to remember longer pieces of music; about metre.
- Section 8 – to respond physically to music with understanding of musical features.

Scottish attainment targets

Using materials, techniques, skills and media (voice/instruments)

- Level C – Sing together confidently in unison producing good vocal tone and clear pronunciation.
- Level D – Play confidently, sustaining more challenging rhythms.

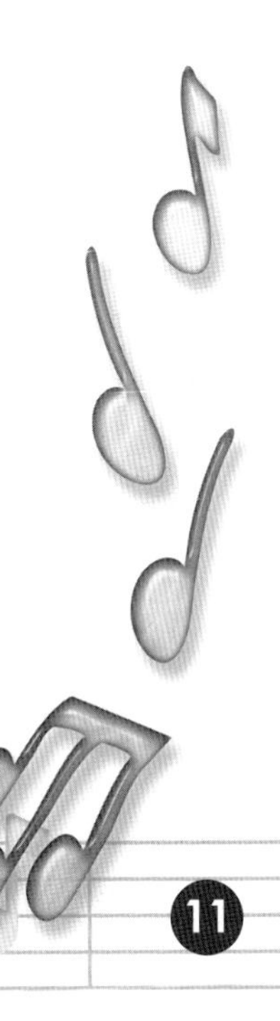

Self advocacy

Lesson 3

Singing techniques

1 Carry out a vocal warm-up by forming a circle and starting with the 'sirens', reminding the children to put their hands on their heads. Count to three and start them off. Now add the 'Tarzan call', where pupils imitate the 'Tarzan' cry, gently drumming their upper chest with their hands in a fist shape.

2 Listen to TRACK 14 on the CD. This is a more advanced vocal exercise, stretching the vocal range higher and lower, louder and softer. Lead the children in repeating the phrases sung in the spaces left in the track for their response.

3 Follow the call-and-answer exercises on TRACK 3. Remind the children that to get higher notes they need to take the sounds up and back into the head and open their mouths wide.

4 Play TRACK 1 and sing along. Ask the children if it is easier to sing after the advanced warm-up.

5 Play TRACK 13, which is the bridge and rap section, a couple of times to enable the children to learn it. Encourage them to have some fun and ask anyone if they know any movements that go along with rapping. Make out you're so old and out of date that the kids will be teaching you something here! Try to imitate their movements and ask them if you got it right. Let them laugh at you a little bit ... but only a little bit.

Lesson 3 Singing techniques

6 Split the class into two groups, and have each in turn stand up and perform the song, using TRACK 2 (the backing track). Ask them to see which group can sing the loudest.

7 Have the two groups perform again, this time with their movements. Remind the children to applaud each other when they have finished performing.

Chill out time!

Have the children sit down at their desks. Each child should lay their head on their arms with eyes closed, breathing slowly through their nose. Challenge them to sit in silence for one minute. Ask the children to think about what would be their dream job – pop star? Hollywood great? Sports hero? Ask them what skills would be necessary for that job and to think about whether or not they have those skills. Finally, ask them to consider what they are good at. After a short while ask the children to sit up and to volunteer to share their ideas with the rest of the class.

Self advocacy

Lesson 4 The rap

Music objective

Learning the rap section of the song and writing their own section.

Learning activity

- Recapping verses, choruses and middle (QCA unit 15:1).
- Recapping rap section from last week (QCA unit 15:7).
- Writing their own rap (QCA unit 21:6).

QCA learning objectives

Unit 15 Ongoing skills

'This unit highlights the musical skills that require regular practice and ongoing development throughout the key stage.'
'Singing songs with control and using the voice expressively.'

- Section 1 – Children should learn about breathing, dynamics and accuracy of pitch.

'Listening, memory and movement.'

- Section 7 – Children should learn to listen with sustained concentration; to remember longer pieces of music; about metre.

Unit 21 Exploring musical processes

'This unit provides an opportunity for children to develop and demonstrate the musical skills, knowledge and understanding achieved in Years 5 and 6.'
'Composing music to a specific brief.'

- Section 6 – Children should learn to use different starting points to create a composition.

Scottish attainment targets

Expressing feelings, ideas, thought and solutions

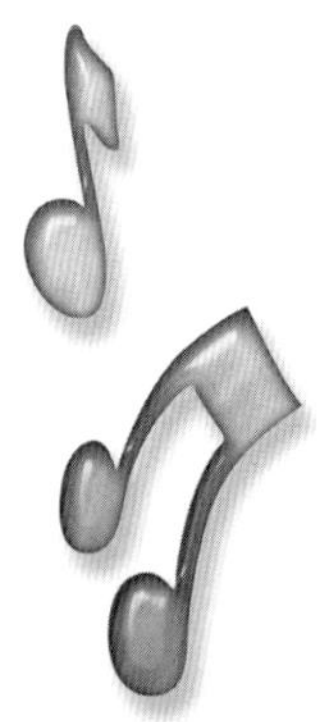

- Level C – Create sound pictures which convey mood and atmosphere; devise a simplified form of notation to represent inventions visually.
- Level D – Invent music which incorporates simple melodic and rhythmic features and shows some awareness of structures, and the ability to select appropriate sound sources.

Evaluating and appreciating

- Level D – Discuss the effect of the use of particular instruments on the mood and character of music.

Self advocacy

Lesson 4 The rap

1 Lead the class in a class warm-up. Form a circle and place hands on heads and make the siren sounds. Next repeat the 'Tarzan' cry, drumming the upper chest gently with fists. Finally, after the count of 3, have everyone stamp forward and shout 'HA', pulling their elbows as they stamp. Repeat with 'HO' and 'HEE'.

2 Play the song through on TRACK 1 and sing along together.

3 Now play the bridge and rap section on TRACK 13 and have everyone rap along.

4 Ask the children to suggest words or phrases related to the theme of the song and write these up on the whiteboard – scribble all over the board, but try to arrange them roughly in groups of similar rhyming words. Try to leave the ideas shouted out in the exact wording that the children express.

5 Using this 'rhyme board', encourage the children to try to come up with four more lines for the rap – see if they can find meaningful phrases using the rhyme word at the end of each line. This way, children will associate words and feelings and most importantly their own expression. For example: 'I wanna be an astronaut, fly to Jupiter or Mars … I wanna be a driver and race around in cars'.

6 Now try the completed rap section, playing TRACK 2, and add your new section at the end. If the children have trouble writing the new lines, leave it out and continue the lesson.

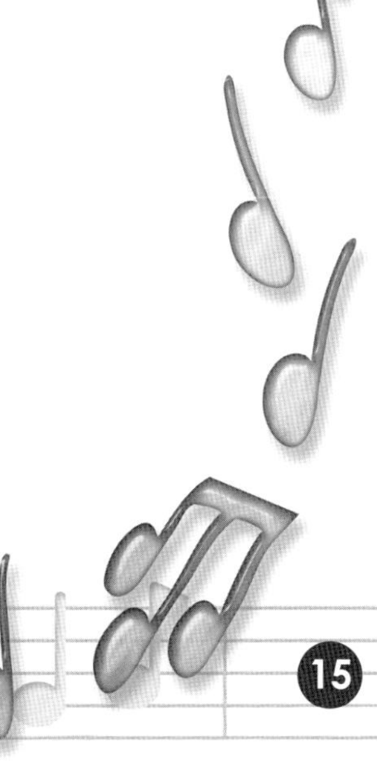

The rap

7 Next, collect all the percussion instruments and recap the pulse and rhythm arrangement on TRACKS 8 and 9.

8 Play, sing and rap through the song, using TRACK 1.

9 Play the pulse on TRACK 8 (you can loop it on the CD player to keep it going for as long as you need it). Ask groups of four or five pupils at a time to try rapping the song rap, then their own rap, against the beat, adding in their movements if they like.

10 Play TRACK 2 (the backing track) for the children to sing and rap along. Experiment using a smaller group (just boys, for example) for the rap, making sure everyone joins the song promptly after the rap section. If the children can't quite manage the song all the way through just yet, use TRACK 1 with the voice for support.

Chill out time!

Have the children sit down at their desks. Each child should lay their head on their arms with eyes closed, breathing slowly through their nose. Encourage them to keep silent and listen to the sounds around them. After two minutes, ask the pupils to think about what ordinary/everyday job they would like to do. Tell them to think realistically about what they would like to be when they grow up.

Self advocacy

Lesson 5 Moods and feelings

Note – You will be using the instrument trolley for this lesson.

Music objective

Exploring musical processes.

Learning activity

- Composing music using a range of different sounds and musical ideas in response to a task set by Music Works (QCA units 21:1, 21:2, 21:6 and 19:6).
- Recapping song (QCA unit 15:7).
- Recapping percussion parts (QCA unit 15:7).

QCA learning objectives

Unit 15 Ongoing skills

'This unit highlights the musical skills that require regular practice and ongoing development throughout the key stage.'
'Listening, memory and movement.'

- Section 7 – Children should learn to listen with sustained concentration; to remember longer pieces of music; about metre.

Unit 19 Songwriter – Exploring lyrics and melody

'This unit develops children's ability to compose a song with an awareness of the relationship between lyrics and melody.'
'How can we compose our own song?'

- Section 6 – Children should learn about writing songs.

Unit 21 Exploring musical processes

'This unit provides an opportunity for children to develop and demonstrate the musical skills, knowledge and understanding achieved in Years 5 and 6.'
'How do composers begin to compose?'

- Section 1 – Children should learn how music is composed from a variety of different stimuli.

'What different starting points can be used to stimulate composition?'

- Section 2 – Children should learn how sounds can be used descriptively.

'Composing music to a specific brief.'

- Section 6 – Children should learn to use different starting points to create a composition.

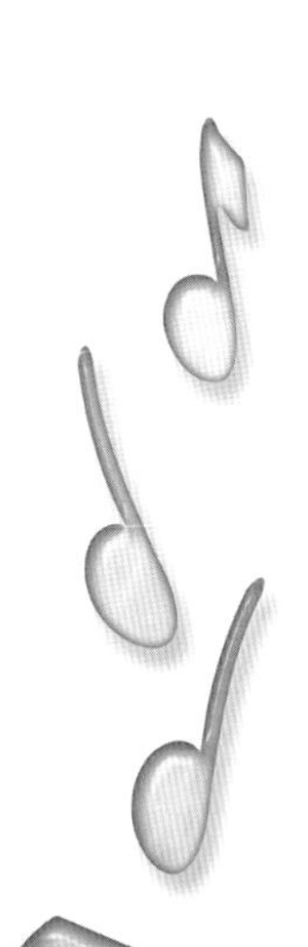

Scottish attainment targets

Expressing feelings, ideas, thoughts and solutions (creating and designing)

- Level D – Invent music which incorporates simple melodic and rhythmic features and shows imagination and some awareness of structures; represent inventions visually in a simplified form of notation.

Self advocacy

Lesson 5 Moods and feelings

1 In this lesson, we leave the song temporarily and explore music in another way. Ask the children to sit in a circle and be quiet. Tell them they are going to listen to three pieces of music and will have to answer questions on it.

2 Play TRACKS 10, 11 and 12 on the CD and listen to the three musical sections. Ask the children which one describes a car mechanic, which a wrestler and which a ballet dancer.

3 Having established that, split the class in to three groups and give out musical instruments.

4 Ask each group to create a short musical piece based on one of the three personas; don't tell the other groups which one they decide to interpret. Spend time with each group and encourage them to try different instruments.

5 Have each group perform their short piece to the other groups and ask the others to guess which character is being portrayed.

6 Return to the song – play TRACK 9 and recap the rhythm parts to the song.

7 Play TRACK 1 and sing and rap along. Ask the children to play percussion at the relevant section. Remember to include movements selected for the rap part and ask all those not rapping in that section to bob down on one knee, in order to give a dynamic to the visual performance. Once the rap part is over, they can quickly stand and sing as soon as the chorus comes in.

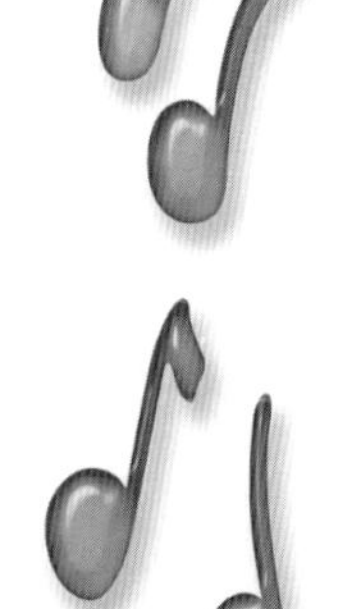

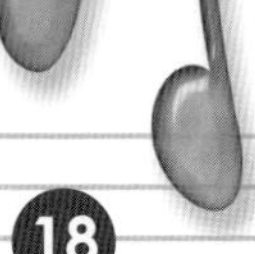

Lesson 5 Moods and feelings

8 Practise the song again with TRACK 1.

9 Now try performing the song against TRACK 2 (the backing track). Repeat this a few times, making sure everyone knows where each different section starts.

10 If there is any time left, ask the children if anyone would like to perform a chorus or verse solo in front of the class. Remember to get everyone to clap even if there are faults – it's important to applaud the effort someone has made to stand up and perform.

Chill out time!

Have the children lie down and relax on the floor, closing their eyes and breathing slowly. Try to induce total silence. Ask the children to listen to the sounds around them. After a suitable amount of time, ask the children to sit up again, then go round the class one by one, asking each child to recount the different sounds they heard. Answers might include: the sound of someone breathing; the distant sound of cars or traffic; birds outside; voices from the classroom next door; someone in the room giggling.

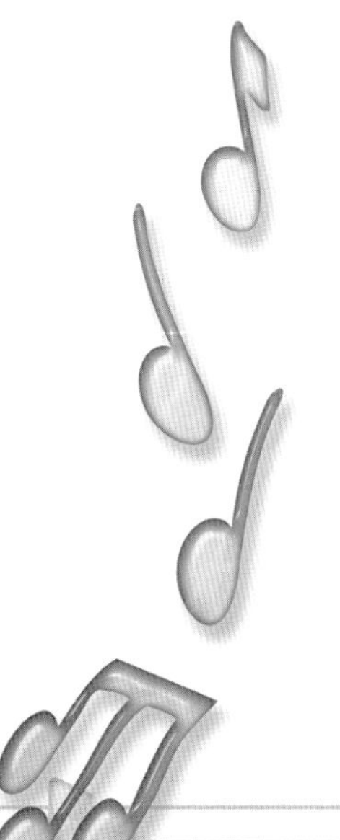

Self advocacy

Lesson 6 The performance

Music objective

Developing the ability to take part in a class performance with confidence, expression and control.

Learning activity

- Performing together (QCA units 15:1, 15:7 and 20:1).
- Playing percussion parts (QCA unit 16:4).
- Doing a vocal warm-up (QCA unit 15:1).

QCA learning objectives

Unit 15 Ongoing skills

'This unit highlights the musical skills that require regular practice and ongoing development throughout the key stage.'

'Singing songs with control and using the voice expressively.'

- Section 1 – Children should learn about breathing, dynamics and accuracy of pitch.

'Listening, memory and movement.'

- Section 7 – Children should learn to listen with sustained concentration; to remember longer pieces of music; about metre.

Unit 16 Cyclic patterns – Exploring rhythm and pulse

'This unit develops pupils' ability to perform rhythmic patterns confidently and with a strong sense of pulse.'

'How can different sounds be used rhythmically?'

- Section 4 – Children should learn about particular cyclic patterns.

Unit 20 Stars, hide your fires – performing together

'This unit develops and demonstrates children's ability to take part in a class performance with confidence, expression and control.'

'What is the song about?'

- Section 1 – Children should learn about the context of the song selected.

Scottish attainment targets

Expressing feelings, ideas, thought and solutions (communicating and presenting)

- Levels A–E – When and where appropriate, present and perform music to the teacher, another group, the rest of the class or a wider audience.

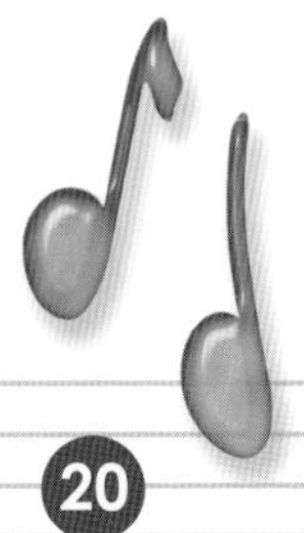

Self advocacy

Lesson 6 The performance

1 The performance can be limited to the classroom. It can be later performed at a school assembly or included in a school play. Note that you will be using TRACK 2 (the backing track) for the performance.

2 Guide the children through a warm-up, as in Lesson 3. Can the children suggest any other warm-up activities?

3 Practise the bridge and rap part first, using TRACK 13 on the CD.

4 Run through the choruses and harmonies using TRACKS 4 and 5.

5 Prepare all the percussion instruments and run through the percussion parts, playing TRACK 9 if necessary. Invite questions from anyone who still isn't sure of what they're doing.

6 Arrange the children into their performing positions. For example, they could stand in two rows, slightly curved in at the ends (a horseshoe shape).

7 Have the children perform the song as well as possible. Children often do their best rendition the first time through, so if you are going to get the children to perform in front of others, try not to let them sing it all the way through, just refresh sections beforehand. Or sing along quietly to TRACK 1 and then TRACK 2.

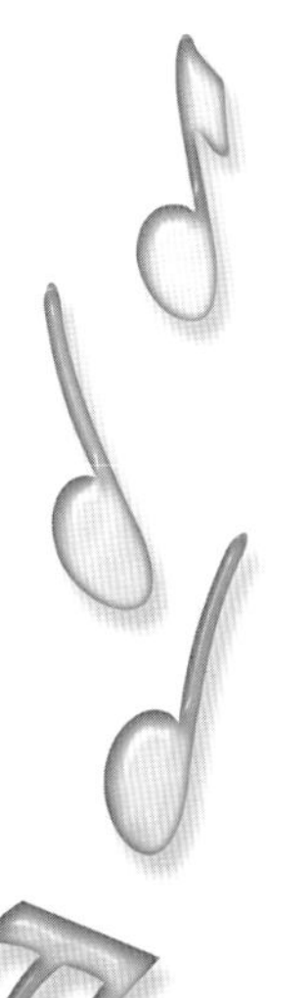

The performance

8 For fun let half the class perform to the other half and then swap over, or boys to girls then girls to boys. The half listening are allowed to pull faces and try to 'put off' the performers but they must not make a sound. This leads to stifled laughter and a great deal of fun. Explain to the children the reason for this is so they may get used to performing in front of people without being 'put off'. It can lead to a strengthening in concentration.

9 Remind the children of the movements they have worked out for their performance, and any other special instructions (for example, if there is going to be a small group performing the rap, what the others are to do while they are listening, and when they must all join in again).

Chill out time!

Use any of the examples in previous lessons or ask the children which 'chill out' they would like to do (for example, the fantasy job, the sounds around them or the realistic job). Ask if anyone has a new idea of things to think about or things to make mental lists of.

Follow your Heart

Verse 1
You've got to follow your heart.
Follow your heart.
Hope it means
You've got the courage to follow your dreams.
Hope, and pray, that light will guide your way.

Chorus
You've got to follow your heart.
Follow your heart.
Follow your heart, oh yeah! (All x2)

Bridge
Everybody's good at something:
What's your thing? What's it gonna be?
Get to the heart of your thing.
Let's hear it, just a little bit.

Rap
If you don't find numbers problematic,
Then go get jiggy with some mathematics.
If music makes your heart beat a little faster,
Then pump up the volume on your ghetto blaster.
If poetry makes you feel more snappy,
Read those rhymes, keep your teacher happy.
If souped-up cars make you ecstatic,
Then get on down and be a car mechanic.

Rap gap

Middle 8
Have your dreams and fascination,
Make your dreams a realisation,
In this world you don't get a free meal:
You got to work hard to make it real.

Verse 2
You've got to follow your heart.
Follow your heart.
Hope it means
You've got the courage to follow your dreams.
Hope, and pray, that light will guide your way.

Chorus
You've got to follow your heart.
Follow your heart.
Follow your heart, oh yeah! (All x2)

GOOD LUCK WITH YOUR PERFORMANCE!
(Note: This performance can take place in the classroom, in front of the whole school at assembly, or as part of a school play. Wherever you perform it, make sure you all have fun doing it!)

Lesson 1 The song: 'Family Tree'

Music objective

Introducing the song and learning parts of it.

Learning activity

- Vocal warm-up (QCA units 15:1–6).
- Building on vocal techniques and building confidence in singing (QCA units15:1–6).
- Following and learning the verses and choruses in the new song (QCA unit 15:7–8).

QCA learning objectives

Unit 15 Ongoing skills

'This unit highlights the musical skills that require regular practice and ongoing development throughout the key stage.'
'Singing songs with control and using the voice expressively.'
Children should learn:

- Section 1 – about breathing, dynamics and accuracy of pitch.
- Section 2 – how to improve tone production and use diction and other vocal techniques, for example legato and staccato.
- Section 3 – about pulse, rhythm and metre.
- Section 4 – about phrase and other musical structures.
- Section 5 – to extend their control and understanding of pitch.
- Section 6 – how to make expressive use of elements and techniques and develop their performances.

'Listening, memory and movement.'
Children should learn:

- Section 7 – to listen with sustained concentration; to remember longer pieces of music; about metre.
- Section 8 – to respond physically to music with understanding of musical features.

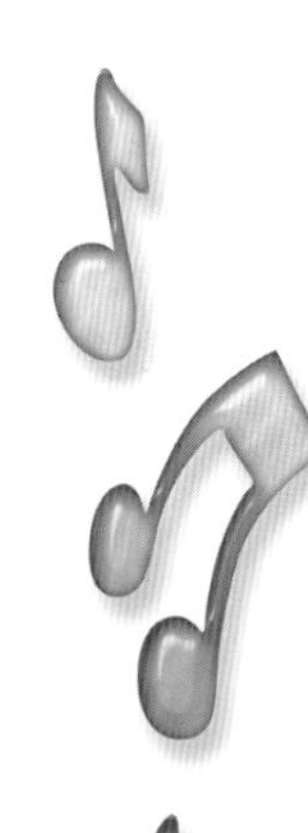

Scottish attainment targets

Using materials, techniques, skills and media (voice)

- Level B – Show a greater ability to sing in tune with others; fit words to the melody where this is obvious.
- Level C – sing together confidently in unison with some awareness of dynamics.

Evaluating and appreciating

- Level C – Demonstrate aural retention; give opinions of own music making and that of others.

Lesson 1 The song: 'Family Tree'

1 Play TRACK 15 on the CD – 'Family Tree'. Listen to it a second time, pointing out the arrangement: the verses, choruses and rap section.

2 Carry out a vocal warm-up. This should be a good fun time. Children should form a circle and stand with hands on heads. On the count of three, ask the children to make sounds imitating police sirens or ambulances. Tell the children that, as the siren sound goes up, they need to let the mouth open wide so that the chin feels nice and relaxed. Finally, ask the children to sigh, letting out any stressful thoughts. After two or three sighs, hold on to the end of the sigh and continue to make that sound as long as possible. Whoever can make it last longest gets a house point (or a point for the class reward system)!

3 Now sing along with TRACK 17 on the CD, to enable the children to learn the melody for the verses. Listen to TRACK 15 again, concentrating on learning the chorus. Listen to the track one more time and learn the middle section. The children should try to memorise the lyrics in the classroom, but they could also take the lyric sheet home to learn or to sing with their friends in the playground during break time.

4 Check out the rap on TRACK 25 but don't worry about learning this today!

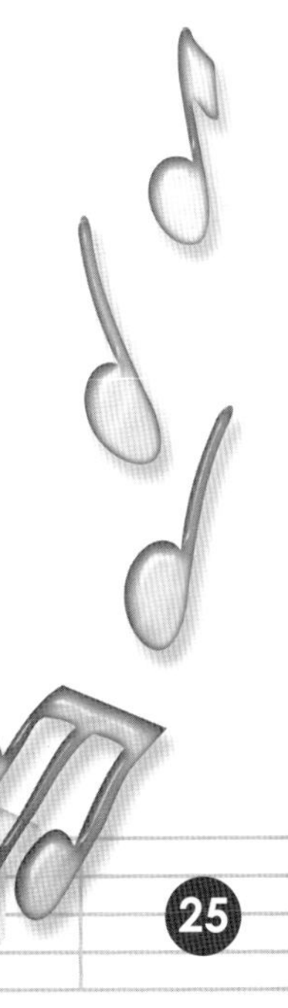

Lesson 1 The song: 'Family Tree'

5 Listen to the vocal exercises on TRACK 18, which take the voice up high and down low. Encourage the children to sing in the gaps left for responses.

6 Invite the children to volunteer to sing the chorus in front of the rest of the class – they could do this in pairs or groups of three if they prefer. Boys in the class might need particular encouragement for this – but don't push them too hard. Praise those boys that do volunteer.

7 Divide the class into two groups and have them perform the song in turn, and see who can sing the loudest. Remind the group listening to applaud the performers.

Chill out time!

Let the children sit back at their desks and relax by resting their heads and closing their eyes. Tell them to sit in silence and listen for the sounds around them. After a minute, ask them to open their eyes and share with the others all the different things they have heard (ask for volunteers to put up their hands). Did anybody hear something that no one else heard?

Lesson 2 The rhythm

Note – You will be using the percussion trolley for this lesson.

Music objective

Becoming aware of structure, and confidently playing pulse and rhythm parts.

Learning activity

- Playing percussion (rhythm and pulse) (QCA unit 16:2).
- Remembering the chorus/verse and middle section of a song (QCA unit 15:7).
- Recapping the basic techniques for building confidence in singing (QCA unit 15:1).

QCA learning objectives

Unit 15 Ongoing skills

'This unit highlights the musical skills that require regular practice and ongoing development throughout the key stage.'

'Singing songs with control and using the voice expressively.'

- Section 1 – Children should learn about breathing, dynamics and accuracy of pitch.

'Listening, memory and movement.'

- Section 7– Children should learn to listen with sustained concentration; to remember longer pieces of music; about metre.

Unit 16 Cyclic patterns – Exploring rhythm and pulse

'This unit develops pupils' ability to perform rhythmic patterns confidently and with a strong sense of pulse.'

'How does some music use cyclic patterns?'

- Section 2 – Children should learn that percussion instruments can produce a wide range of sound.

Scottish attainment targets

Using materials, techniques, skills and media (instruments)

- Level B – Play simple rhythmic patterns showing control over speed and volume.
- Level C – Display two-handed co-ordination in playing straightforward melodies and rhythms.
- Level D – Play confidently on a range of instruments.

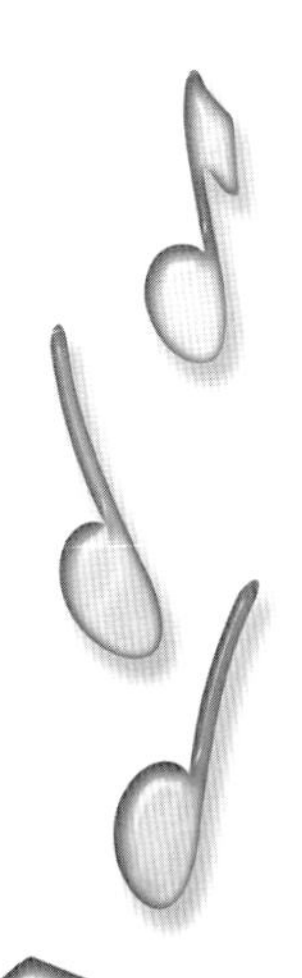

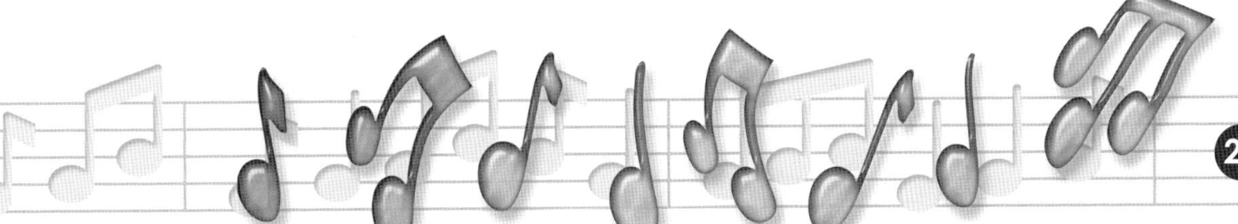

Lesson 2 The rhythm

1. Play TRACK 15 on the CD and sing along gently.
2. Listen to TRACK 20, which plays the pulse – clap along with it and count 1, 2, 3, 4. Point out to the children that this is a steady regular beat, giving the tempo or speed of the music.
3. Listen to the rhythm on TRACK 21. Encourage the children to hear how it's different to the pulse and the beats are not evenly spaced as before, and how it fits in well with the pulse. Challenge them to suggest another rhythm that would also fit.
4. Split the class in half and have one section clap the pulse while the other section claps the rhythm.
5. Hand out percussion instruments and ask the children with tambourines to play the pulse and those with woodblocks to play the rhythm.
6. Now play along with TRACK 15 with percussion in two parts.
7. Guide the children through the sirens part of the warm-up. Now sing along with the song to refresh the memory. The children should sing gently at first; it's more important to make sure the voices are clear and words are sung with heartfelt expression.

Lesson 2 The rhythm

8 Sing the song again, but this time adding the percussion at the relevant part of the arrangement.

9 Have the children stand and sing through the song to TRACK 15, then see if they can perform against TRACK 16 (the backing track), without the voice for support. Encourage them to try to make it through to the end.

10 Discuss with the children how they would like the song to end. For example, they could get as loud as possible for a big finish. Alternatively, they could get progressively quieter over the last three or four lines so they finish on a whisper.

Chill out time!

Repeat the listening game from Lesson 1, only this time ask the children to find enough space on the floor to lie down and close their eyes, relax and listen for different sounds.

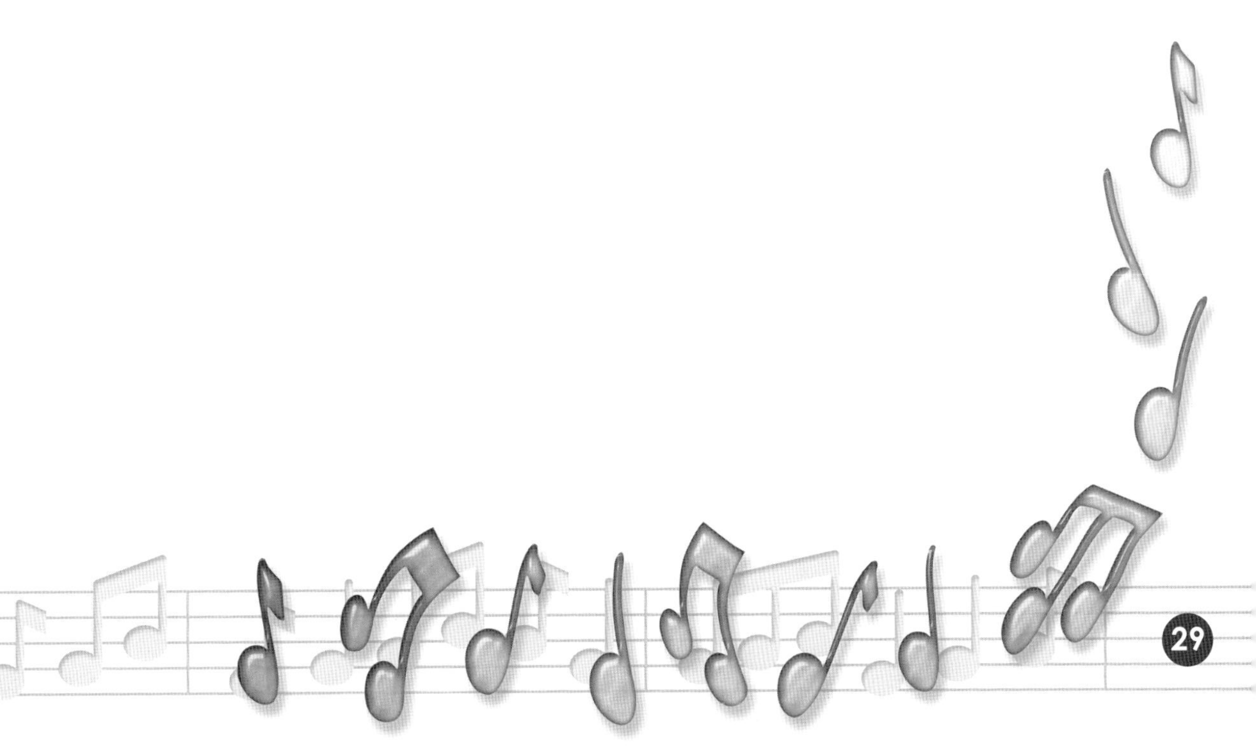

Lesson 3 Singing techniques

Music objective

Improve vocal quality and learn the rap section of the song.

Learning activity

- Full vocal warm-up (QCA unit 15:1).
- Stretching the voice further (QCA unit 15:1).
- Recapping verses and choruses (QCA unit 15:7).
- Learning the rap section (QCA units 15:7–8).

QCA learning objectives

Unit 15 Ongoing skills

'This unit highlights the musical skills that require regular practice and ongoing development throughout the key stage.'
'Singing songs with control and using the voice expressively.'

- Section 1 – Children should learn about breathing, dynamics and accuracy of pitch.

'Listening, memory and movement.'
Children should learn:

- Section 7 – to listen with sustained concentration; to remember longer pieces of music; about metre.
- Section 8 – to respond physically to music with understanding of musical features.

Scottish attainment targets

Using materials, techniques, skills and media (voice)

- Level C – Sing together confidently in unison, with some awareness of dynamics, phrasing and expression.

Expressing feelings, ideas, thought and solutions

- Level D – Invent music which incorporates simple rhythmic features and show imagination and some awareness of structures.

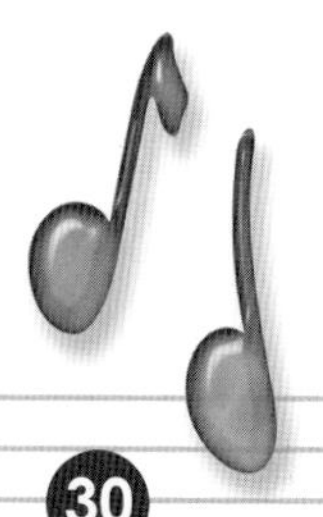

Lesson 3 Singing techniques

1 Lead the children in a full vocal warm-up as in Lesson 1.

- Ask the children to form a circle and relax.
- Tell them to let out a big sigh, then repeat but this time, on the count of three, to hold on to the last note in the sigh. As they sigh, have the children droop to the ground as they finish sighing. Last one standing gets a point!
- Standing in the circle, ask the children to make circular movements with their arms bent, elbows making circles away from the chest, opening the upper chest and stretching the muscles gently.
- Next, to get the chest voice going, tell the children to stamp forward after the count of three and shout 'ha', pulling back their elbows as they stamp, then repeating with different vowel sounds: 1, 2, 3, 'HA'; 1, 2, 3, 'HO'; 1, 2, 3, 'HEE'. Now string it together: 1, 2, 3, 'HA', 2, 3, 'HO', 2, 3, 'HEE', 2, 3 and so on. They should do this six times or so.

2 Add in the 'Tarzan call', where pupils imitate the 'Tarzan' cry, gently drumming their upper chest with hands in a fist shape.

3 Listen to TRACK 18 on the CD. This is a more advanced vocal exercise, stretching the vocal range higher and lower, louder and softer. Lead the children in repeating the phrases in the gaps left for their response.

4 Ask the children to follow the call-and-answer exercises on TRACK 19, which focuses on vowels and vocalising.

5 Remind the children that, to get higher notes, they need to take the sounds up and back in to the head and open their mouths wide.

6 Play TRACK 15 and encourage the class to sing along. Ask them if it is easier to sing after the advanced warm-up.

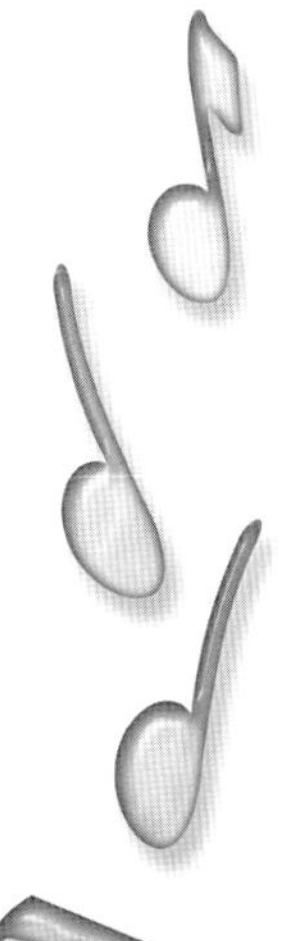

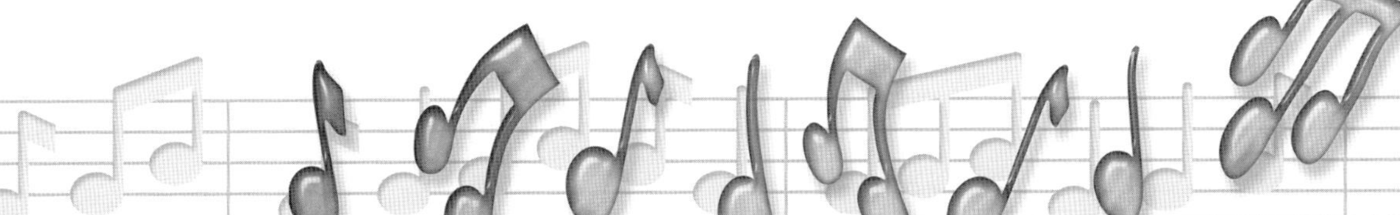

Lesson 3 Singing techniques

7 Play TRACK 25 (the rap section) a few times to help the children to learn it. Have some fun and ask anyone if they know any movements that go along with rapping. Make out you're so old and out of date that the kids will be teaching you something here! Try to imitate their movements and ask them if you got it right. Let them laugh at you a little bit … but only a little bit!

8 Play TRACK 16 (the backing track) and see if the children can sing through to the end without making any big mistakes.

9 Ask the children now to focus on their words and on making them very clear so their audience can understand them. Just for fun, sing the first part of the song up to the rap with really exaggerated mouth movements.

10 Perform the song once more, but with volunteers singing some parts solo or in small groups. Make sure the children listening encourage and applaud those brave enough to stand up and perform.

Chill out time!

Ask the children to find a space on the floor and lie down; instruct them to relax, close their eyes and not speak. Ask them to imagine they are a big sack of potatoes: the sides of the sack have split open and all the potatoes are rolling out. Tell them to relax the toes, the feet, the legs, the body, the arms and the head. When the children have relaxed for a suitable period, ask them to roll up from the head first into a sitting position.

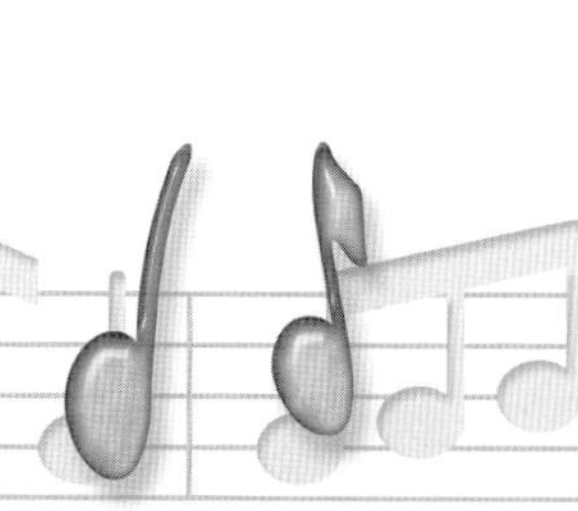

Lesson 4 The rap

Note – You will be using the percussion trolley for this lesson.

Music objective

Learning the rap section of the song and writing their own section.

Learning activity

- Recapping verses, choruses and middle (QCA unit 15:7).
- Recapping rap section from the previous lesson (QCA unit 15:7).
- Writing their own rap (QCA unit 19:1 and 19:6).
- Deciding on appropriate movements (QCA unit 15:8).

QCA learning objectives

Unit 15 Ongoing skills

'This unit highlights the musical skills that require regular practice and ongoing development throughout the key stage.'
'Singing songs with control and using the voice expressively.'
Children should learn:

- Section 7 – to listen with sustained concentration; to remember longer pieces of music; about metre.
- Section 8 – to respond physically to music with understanding of musical features.

Unit 19 Songwriter – Exploring lyrics and melody

'This unit develops children's ability to compose a song with an awareness of the relationship between lyrics and melody.'
'How does a song use lyrics?'

- Section 1 – Children should learn what is meant by the term 'lyrics' and how they can reflect the time and place in which they were written.

'How are music and lyrics used together in songs?'

- Section 6 – Children should learn how lyrics can be generated and organised.

Scottish attainment targets

Expressing feelings, ideas, thought and solutions

- Level C – Create sound phrases that convey mood and atmosphere.
- Level D – Invent music which incorporates simple melodic and rhythmic features and shows some awareness of structures and the ability to select appropriate sound sources.

Evaluating and appreciating

- Level D – Discuss the effect of the use of particular instruments on the mood and character of music.

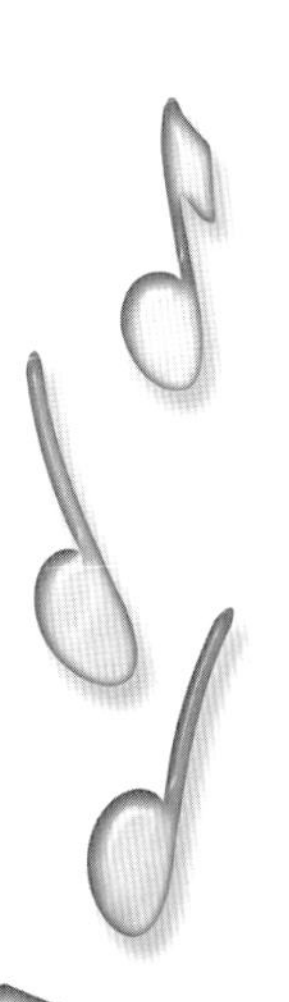

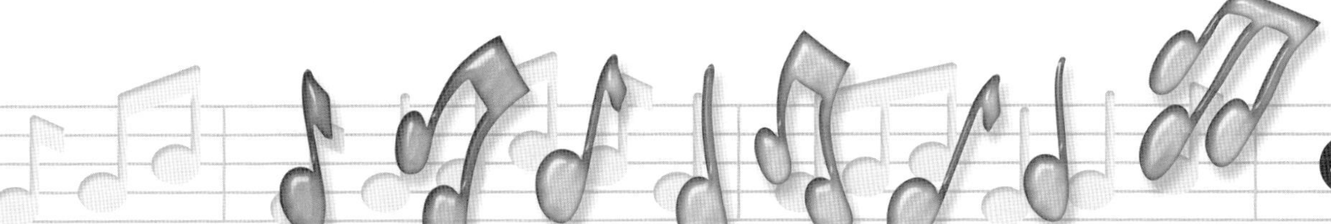

Lesson 4 The rap

1 See if the children can carry out a warm-up by themselves. Do they remember how they did it in previous lessons?

2 Play through the song on TRACK 15, followed by the rap section on TRACK 25.

3 Ask the children to suggest words or phrases related to the theme of the song, and write these up on the whiteboard – scribble all over the board, but try to arrange them roughly in groups of similar rhyming words. Ask them to think of their own family members (for example their sister, brother, grandmother and so on), and whether they have any special names for them such as 'nan' or 'gran'. Encourage them then to find rhymes for these words. Ask them to think about where these people live, whether in the same house or street or far away. Expand this then to have the children consider the other families in their neighbourhood and the worries that any family might have, such as paying the bills or behaviour towards each other. Try to leave the ideas shouted out in the exact wording that the children express.

4 Encourage the children to use this 'rhyme board' to come up with four more lines for the rap – see if they can find meaningful phrases using the rhyme word at the end of each line. This way children will associate words and feelings and most importantly their own expression.

5 Next, have the children try the completed rap section; play TRACK 25 to help them.

6 Ask the children to collect the percussion instruments and recap with them the pulse and rhythm arrangement on TRACKS 20 and 21.

Lesson 4 The rap

7 Play, sing and rap through the song, playing TRACK 15 to help. Then perform the song again, this time using TRACK 16 (the backing track).

8 Divide the class into two groups (perhaps boys and girls, or according to birthdays or the letters beginning their names) and have just one group perform the rap. Boys will often be happier about rapping than singing, so this could be their chance to shine (although do keep encouraging them to sing as well).

9 Have each group perform the whole song to the other group, and compete to see who can do it the loudest.

Chill out time!

Ask the children to find a space and lie down, then stretch out, close their eyes and relax. Ask them to think for a short while and imagine a place where they would like to live – is it the countryside? Beside the sea? Somewhere else entirely? After two or three minutes, ask the children to sit up slowly and go round the class selecting children to say what place they had imagined.

Lesson 5 Moods and feelings

Note – You will be using the percussion trolley for this lesson.

Music objective

Exploring musical processes.

Learning activity

- Composing music using a range of different sounds and musical ideas in response to a task set by Music Works (QCA unit 21:6).
- Recapping song (QCA unit 15:7).
- Recapping percussion parts (QCA units 15:7).

QCA learning objectives

Unit 15 Ongoing skills

'This unit highlights the musical skills that require regular practice and ongoing development throughout the key stage.'
'Listening, memory and movement.'

- Section 7– Children should learn to listen with sustained concentration; to remember longer pieces of music; about metre.

Unit 21 Exploring musical processes

'This unit provides an opportunity for children to develop and demonstrate the musical skills, knowledge and understanding achieved in Years 5 and 6.'
'Bringing it all together: Composing music to a given brief.'

- Section 6 – Children should learn to use different starting points to create a composition.

Scottish attainment targets

Expressing feelings, ideas, thought and solutions (creating and designing)

- Level D – Invent music which incorporates simple melodic and rhythmic features and shows some awareness of structures and contrasts; represent inventions visually in a simplified form of notation.

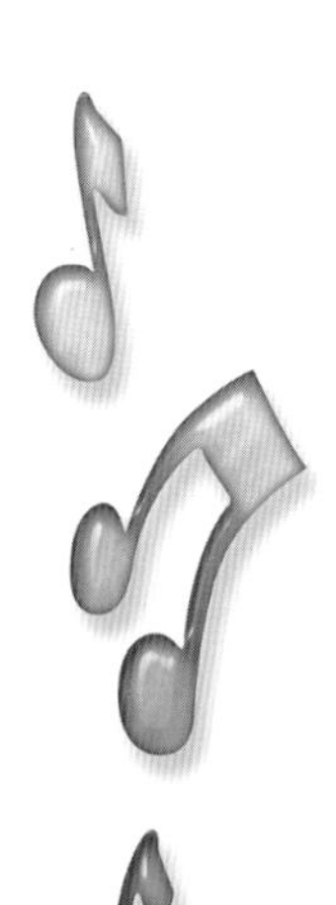

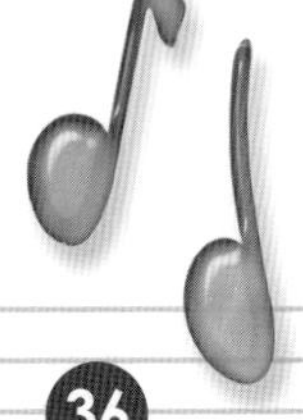

Lesson 5 Moods and feelings

1 In this lesson, we leave the song temporarily and explore music in another way.

2 Ask the children to sit in a circle and remain quiet. Tell them they will listen to three pieces of music and answer questions on them.

3 Play TRACKS 22, 23 and 24 and listen to three musical sections. Ask the children to identify which of the sections evokes the idea of anger/jealousy, which one reminds them of happiness and which piece describes the idea of 'falling in love'.

4 Having established the answers, split the class in to three groups and give out available musical instruments.

5 Ask each group to create a short musical piece describing one of the three emotions: anger/jealousy, happiness, falling in love, but not to tell the other groups which one they decide to interpret.

6 After a short time, ask each group to perform theirs to the other groups and have the others guess which emotion is being portrayed.

7 Return to the main song. Play TRACK 21 and recap the rhythm parts to the song.

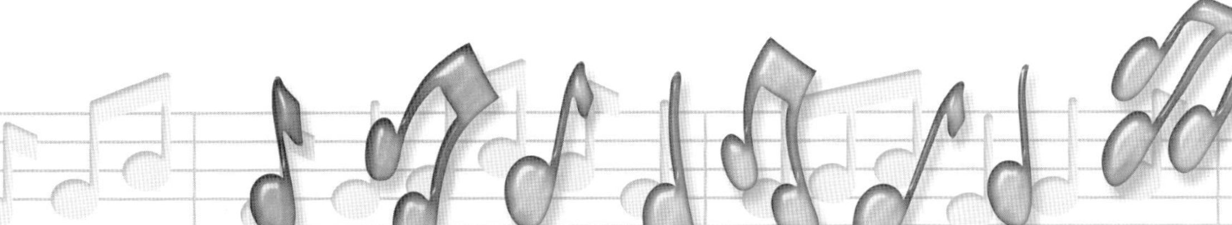

Lesson 5 Moods and feelings

8 Play TRACK 15 and sing and rap along with the class. Before you begin, decide which part of the song the percussion can accompany, and tell the children when it's going to happen. Remember to bring them in as they are singing. Remember to include movements selected for the rap part and ask all those not rapping in that section to bob down on one knee, in order to give a dynamic to the visual performance. Once the rap part is over, they can quickly stand and sing as soon as the chorus comes in.

9 Practise the song again with TRACK 15. Then perform the song with TRACK 16 (the backing track) and see if the children can get all the way through to the end.

10 Remind the children how they had decided to do the ending (soft or loud). Rehearse the ending without a backing track and see how long the children can keep on sustaining the last note.

Chill out time!

Let the children sit back at their desks and relax by resting their heads and closing their eyes. Tell them to sit in silence and listen for the sounds around them. After a minute, ask them to open their eyes and share with the others all the different things they have heard (ask for volunteers to put up their hands). Did anybody hear something that no one else heard? It's best if you can limit it to one sound per child; if there is a repeat, ask that child to remember another sound they heard.

Lesson 6 The performance

Music objective

Developing the ability to take part in a class performance with confidence, expression and control.

Learning activity

- Performing together (QCA units 15:7, 20:2 and 20:6).
- Playing percussion parts (QCA unit 16:2).
- Doing a vocal warm-up (QCA unit 15:7).

QCA learning objectives

Unit 15 Ongoing skills

'This unit highlights the musical skills that require regular practice and ongoing development throughout the key stage.'

'Listening, memory and movement.'

- Section 7– Children should learn to listen with sustained concentration; to remember longer pieces of music; about metre.

Unit 16 Cyclic patterns – Exploring rhythm and pulse

'This unit develops pupils' ability to perform rhythmic patterns confidently and with a strong sense of pulse.'

'How can different sounds be used rhythmically?'

- Section 2 – Children should learn that percussion instruments can produce a wide range of sound.

Unit 20 Stars, hide your fires – performing together

'This unit develops and demonstrates children's ability to take part in a class performance with confidence, expression and control.'

'What is the song about?'

- Section 2 – Children should learn how to improve diction and sing in two parts.

'Bringing it all together.'

- Section 6 – Children should learn how to achieve a high quality performance that creates the intended effect.

Scottish attainment targets

Expressing feelings, ideas, thought and solutions (communicating and presenting)

- Levels A–E – When and where appropriate, present and perform music to the teacher, another group, the rest of the class, or a wider audience.

Evaluating and appreciating

- Levels A–E – Demonstrate awareness of sound and responsiveness to music.

Lesson 6 The performance

1. The performance can be limited to the classroom, or it can be later performed at a school assembly or included in a school play. Note that you will need to use TRACK 16 (the backing track) for the performance.
2. Guide the class in a warm-up. You could ask if any of the children want to lead the class in the warm-up exercise if they feel confident enough.
3. Practise the rap part first by listening to TRACK 25 on the CD.
4. Run through the harmonies using TRACK 15.
5. Get all the percussion instruments ready and run through each part with the children.
6. Play the percussion parts together, using TRACK 21 if necessary.
7. Make sure everyone is standing in the correct places with the correct posture.
8. Next, have the children perform the song as well as possible. Children often do their best rendition the first time through, so if you are going to get the children to perform in front of others, try not to let them sing all of it – just refresh the sections beforehand.

Lesson 6 The performance

9 For fun, let half the class perform to the other half and then swap over, or boys to girls then girls to boys. The half listening are allowed to pull faces and try to 'put off' the performers but they must not make a sound. This leads to stifled laughter and a great deal of fun.

10 For a final run-through, ask the children to imagine that they are performing in front of the whole school, and that all the younger children will be looking up to them and thinking that they are really cool. Encourage them to perform with gusto as they sing through the song with TRACK 16 (the backing track).

Chill out time!

Have the children sit down at their desks. Each child should lay their head on their arms with eyes closed, breathing slowly through their nose. Ask them to listen to the sounds around them and to think about three good things that have happened to them today. Perhaps they are warm and dry, they have had something good to eat, or they have been laughing at something. After a short while ask the children to sit up and open their eyes, and invite volunteers to share their ideas with the rest of the class.

Family Tree

GOOD LUCK WITH YOUR PERFORMANCE!

(Note: This performance can take place in the classroom, in front of the whole school at assembly, or as part of a school play. Wherever you perform it, make sure you all have fun doing it!)

Verse 1
Why in the world are we
Fighting on endlessly?
Picking on one another
'Cos they're not the same as me?

Verse 2
Birds that are in the trees,
Different feathers and breeds,
Hummingbirds soft and gentle,
While the eagle is proud and free.

Chorus
We all live and breathe,
Our colour and our creed
Don't matter much to me.
We're all from the same,
all from the same,
all from the same family tree.

Rap
Blonde hair, red hair, afro sheen,
We're all from the same love machine.
Whether you're able, whether you're not,
We're all from the same melting pot.

Rap gap

Verse 3
Why in the world can't we
Live as one family.
So many branches on just one tree
There's room for us all to grow – endlessly.

Chorus
We all live and breathe,
Our colour and our creed
Don't matter much to me.
We're all from the same,
all from the same,
all from the same family tree.

We all live and breathe,
Our colour and our creed
Don't matter much to me.
We're all from the same,
all from the same,
all from the same family tree.

Lesson 1 The song: 'This Friend of Mine'

Music objective

Introducing the song and learning parts of it.

Learning activity

- Vocal warm-up (QCA units 15:1–6).
- Building on vocal techniques and building confidence in singing (QCA units 15:1–6).
- Following and learning the verses and choruses in the new song (QCA units 8:7).

QCA learning objectives

Unit 15 Ongoing skills

'This unit highlights the musical skills that require regular practice and ongoing development throughout the key stage.'
'Singing songs with control and using the voice expressively.'
Children should learn:

- Section 1 – about breathing, dynamics and accuracy of pitch.
- Section 2 – how to improve tone production and use diction and other vocal techniques, for example legato and staccato.
- Section 3 – about pulse, rhythm and metre.
- Section 4 – about phrase and other musical structures.
- Section 5 – to extend their control and understanding of pitch.
- Section 6 – how to make expressive use of elements and techniques and develop their performances.

Scottish attainment targets

Evaluating and appreciating

- Levels A–E – Demonstrate awareness of sound and responsiveness to music in a variety of styles produced by self and others.

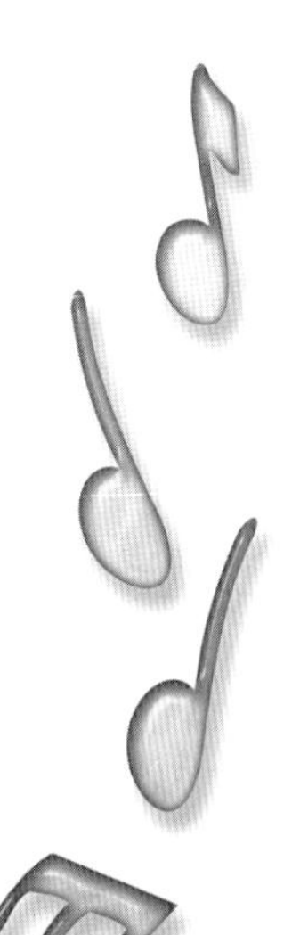

The song: 'This Friend of Mine'

1 Play TRACK 26 on the CD – 'This Friend of Mine'. Listen again, pointing out the arrangement to the children: the opening chorus followed by a verse, a chorus, another verse, a rap then chorus followed by a gap for to the children to add four lines of their own rap, then finishing on a chorus: chorus, verse 1, chorus, verse 2, rap, chorus, rap gap, chorus-out.

2 Ask the children to do a vocal warm-up – see if they can do it without your guidance. This should be a good fun time! Reinforce the information learned in earlier lessons that we sing using our whole body, not just the vocal chords, so we need to make sure we are relaxed and open physically in order to release the voice. Take ten minutes to do the warm-up.

- Children stand in a circle – make sure they are standing in 'neutral' i.e. unfolded arms, legs shoulder-width apart, imagine head attached to string from above, pulling the head and shoulders up straight.
- Loosen up the body in whatever way is preferred (for example rotating the head in a circle, doing large circles clockwise and anti-clockwise with the arms from the shoulder, circles with the hips, circles with the feet, knees, then shaking the whole leg away).
- Take deep breaths into the lower abdomen to the count of 4 through the nose. Now breathe into the upper chest to the next count of 4. Long breaths out to a count of 20. (You could ask children to put their hands on their tummies, so they can feel it rising and falling as they breathe. This ensures diaphragmatic, rather than shallow breaths.)
- Repeat now doing a 'Sss' sound on the out-breath.
- Repeat doing a hum on the out-breath.
- Explain to the children that the diaphragm is a strange-shaped muscle that can be felt if we put our hands just below the ribcage and say a short, sharp 'Cah'. Tell them to do this several times and to see if they can feel their diaphragm moving. Next, ask them to try the same thing, but with their hands on their backs, just above the kidneys, to see if they can feel the diaphragm moving there too. Tell them that, when we sing, we use this muscle as our 'volume pedal' to push the sound out: the harder we push with our diaphragm, the louder the sound. To exercise the diaphragm and therefore build up our singing voices, go through the alphabet (consonants only) to the rhythm of 'Ba, Ba, Ba, Barbaran' (as in the Beach Boys song!), so: 'ba, ba, ba, ba-ba-ba, ba' then 'ca, ca, ca, ca-ca-ca ca', and so on. Whilst they do this, they should keep their hands resting on their belly-button area so they can feel how hard their diaphragm is working.

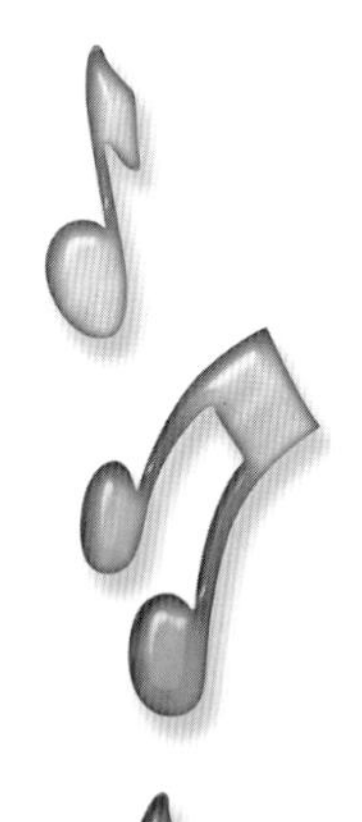

Lesson 1 The song: 'This Friend of Mine'

- Listen and follow TRACK 28 on the CD. The CD guides you through this voice releasing exercise, in the form of call and answer. (Something is shouted on the CD, there is a gap for you to copy this and shout it back. Come in after the count of 4.) The children should push their elbows back in one short movement and, at the same time, release a very loud 'HEY' sound. Point out that normally teachers want children to be quiet, but now you want them to be as loud as they can be.

3 Now sing along with TRACK 29 on the CD, helping the children to learn the chorus.

4 Ask the children to listen out for other voices on the CD and identify what they are doing. Once they have identified that the other voices are singing a harmony, challenge them to see if they can pick out some of the other notes that are being sung. This will allow the children to develop their listening skills.

5 Next listen to TRACK 30 to learn verses 1 and 2.

6 Finally, listen to the rap on TRACK 36, but don't worry about learning this today. Allow anyone who knows how to move to the rap to show the rest of the class, and you, how to move to the beat. Have a laugh!

Chill out time!

Have the children sit down at their desks. Each child should lay their head on their arms with eyes closed, breathing slowly through their nose. Challenge them to sit in total silence. Ask them to think about the sounds around them and to listen out for the different sounds they can hear. After a couple of minutes, have the children sit up and open their eyes, then ask them to name the sounds they heard, going around the class one by one. If someone names a sound that's already been given, make a sound like a klaxon and tell them they have to come up with another.

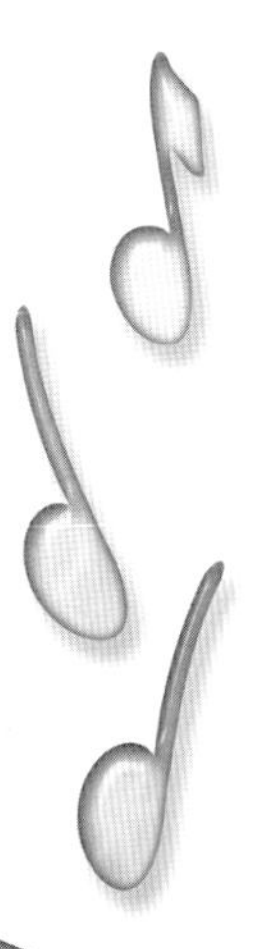

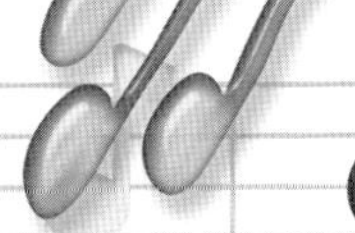

World poverty

Lesson 2

The rhythm

Note – You will be using the percussion trolley for this lesson.

Music objective

Becoming aware of structure and confidently playing pulse and rhythm parts.

Learning activity

- Playing percussion (rhythm and pulse) (QCA units 16:1–4).
- Remembering chorus/verse and middle section of a song (QCA unit 15:7).
- Recapping basic techniques for building confidence in singing (QCA unit 15:1).

QCA learning objectives

Unit 15 Ongoing skills

'This unit highlights the musical skills that require regular practice and ongoing development throughout the key stage.'
'Singing songs with control and using the voice expressively.'

- Section 1 – Children should learn about breathing, dynamics and accuracy of pitch.

'Listening, memory and movement.'

- Section 7 – Children should learn to listen with sustained concentration; to remember longer pieces of music; about metre.

Unit 16 Cyclic patterns – Exploring rhythm and pulse

'This unit develops pupils' ability to perform rhythmic patterns confidently and with a strong sense of pulse.'
'How does some music use cyclic patterns?'

- Section 1 – Children should learn about cyclic patterns.

'How can different sounds be used rhythmically?'
Children should learn:

- Section 2 – that percussion instruments can produce a wide range of sound.
- Section 3 – how different patterns can fit together.
- Section 4 – about particular cyclic patterns.

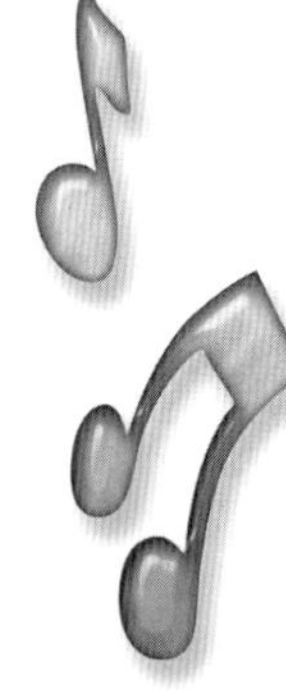

Scottish attainment targets

Using materials, techniques, skills and media (instruments)

- Level B – Play simple rhythmic patterns showing some control over speed and volume.
- Level C – Display two-handed co-ordination in playing straightforward melodies and rhythms.
- Level C – Play confidently on a range of instruments.

Expressing feelings, ideas, thought and solutions

- Level C – Create sound pictures, displaying some imagination with awareness to structure.

Lesson 2 The rhythm

1 Carry out a warm-up as before. See if the children can do it without your guidance.

2 Form a circle and get everyone to clap a steady beat. Ask them 'What did you have for breakfast today?' Have the children reply, one by one, on the beat of the pulse being clapped, and have the rest of the class repeat it after them – so if a child replies 'Toast', then everyone shouts 'TOAST' as loud as possible. If a child is shy and just shakes his or her head, then everyone shakes their head and you move on around the circle to the next child. Avoid dwelling on any one character.

3 Play TRACK 29 on the CD, and have the children sing along gently with the chorus.

4 Listen to TRACK 31, which plays the pulse – clap along with it and count 1, 2, 3 and 4. Point out to the children that this is a steady regular beat, giving us the tempo or speed of the music.

5 Listen to the rhythm on TRACK 32. Ask the children to listen out for how it's different to the pulse and that the beats are not evenly spaced as before, and how it fits in well with the pulse. Challenge them to suggest another rhythm that would also fit with the pulse.

6 Split the class in half and have one section clap the pulse and the other section clap the rhythm. Hand out percussion and ask the children with tambourines to play the pulse and those with woodblocks to play the rhythm. Then have them play along with TRACK 26 with percussion in two parts.

The rhythm

7 Now sing along with the song on TRACK 26 to refresh everyone's memory. Don't be afraid to sing gently at first – it's more important to make sure the voices are clear and words are sung with heartfelt expression.

8 Sing through the song again but this time add the percussion at the relevant part of the arrangement.

9 Play TRACK 27 (the backing track) and see how far the children can sing through the song without getting lost. Remember to bring in the percussion parts where you would like them to happen.

10 Ask if any of the children would like to sing solo in front of the rest of the class – they could perform just a verse or a chorus, and they could sing in pairs if they prefer. Encourage the other children to applaud loudly at the end – remind them it's the effort put into the performance that's important.

Chill out time!

Have the children lie down on the floor, close their eyes and relax in complete silence. After a minute, ask them to think about a breakfast fit for a king. Ask the children to think about what their fantasy breakfast would be, where they would be eating it and who would be there with them. After a few minutes, have the children sit up and then go round the class asking them for their ideas.

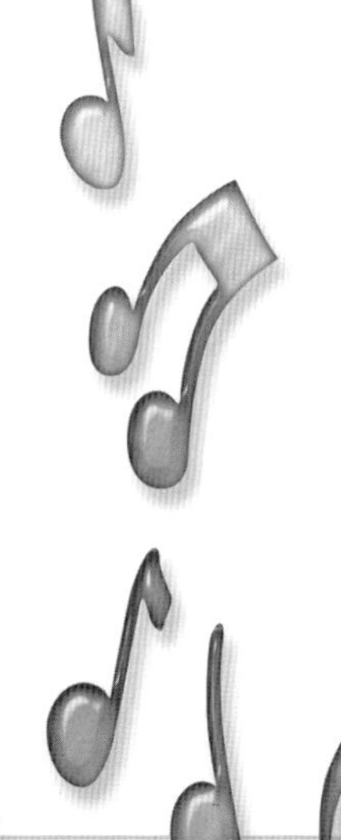

Lesson 3 Singing techniques

Music objective

Improve vocal quality and learn the rap section of the song.

Learning activity

- Full vocal warm-up and stretching voice further (QCA unit 15:1).
- Recapping verses and choruses (QCA unit 15:7).
- Learning rap section (QCA unit 15:8).

QCA learning objectives

Unit 15 Ongoing skills

'This unit highlights the musical skills that require regular practice and ongoing development throughout the key stage.'

'Singing songs with control and using the voice expressively.'

- Section 1 – Children should learn about breathing, dynamics and accuracy of pitch.

'Listening, memory and movement.'

Children should learn:

- Section 7 – to listen with sustained concentration; to remember longer pieces of music; about metre.
- Section 8 – to respond physically to music with understanding of musical features.

Scottish attainment targets

Using materials, techniques, skills and media (voice/instruments)

- Level C – Sing together confidently in unison producing good vocal tone and clear pronunciation.
- Level D – Play confidently, sustaining more challenging rhythms.

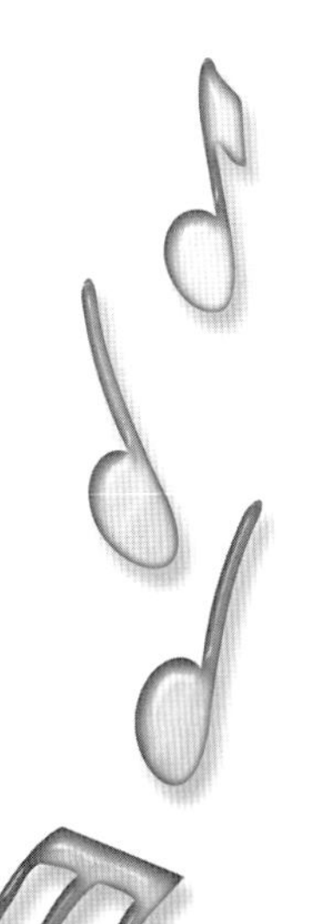

Singing techniques

1. Carry out a vocal warm-up by forming a circle and starting with the 'sirens', reminding the children to put their hands on their heads. Count to three and start them off. Now add the 'Tarzan call', where pupils imitate the 'Tarzan' cry, gently drumming their upper chest with their hands in a fist shape.

2. Listen to TRACK 37 on the CD. This is a more advanced vocal exercise, stretching the vocal range higher and lower, louder and softer.

3. Follow the four call-and-answer exercises on TRACK 28. Remind the children that, to get higher notes, they need to take the sounds up and back into the head and open their mouths wide.

4. Play TRACK 26 and sing along to the song. Ask the children if it is easier to sing after the advanced warm-up.

5. Play TRACK 36, which is the rap section, a couple of times so the children can learn it. Have some fun and ask anyone if they know any movements that go along with rapping. Tell them you can't remember how to do it. Try to imitate their movements and ask them if you got it right.

Lesson 3 Singing techniques

6 Have the children sing along to TRACK 26, stopping just before the rap. Praise their singing, then see if they can do it again but louder. Then see if they can sing it louder still.

7 Go through the same part of the song again (stopping at the rap) but this time to TRACK 27 (the backing track). See if the children can tell where to come in properly. This might need a few attempts to get it right.

8 Split the class into two groups (boys and girls, for example). Have one group perform the first half of the song to the other then swap over and let the other group have a turn. Ask the children which group they thought was the loudest and whether they could understand the words the other group was singing.

Chill out time!

Have the children sit down at their desks. Each child should lay their head on their arms with eyes closed, breathing slowly through their nose. Ask them to think about nothing.

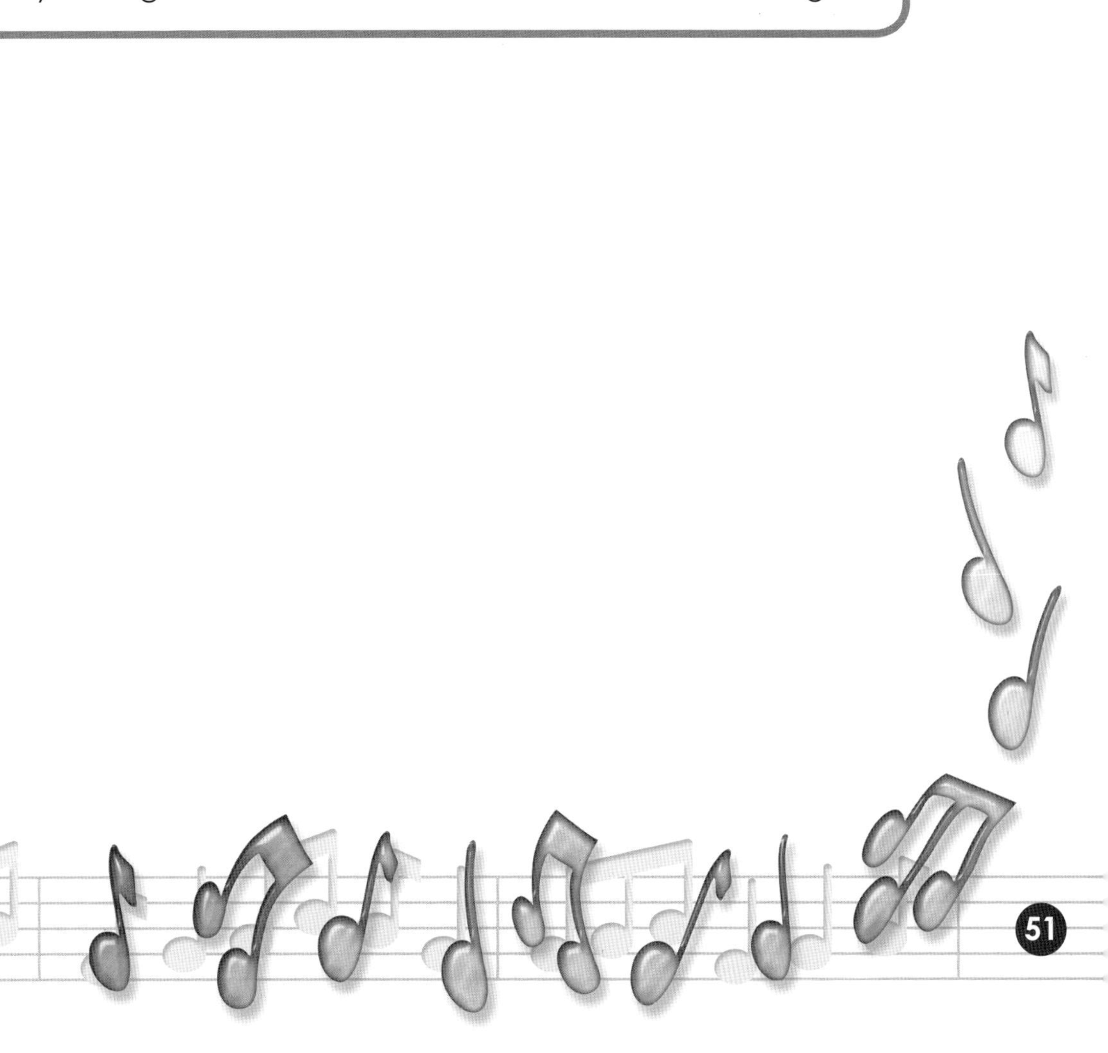

The rap

Note – You will be using the percussion trolley for this lesson.

Music objective

Learning the rap section of the song and writing their own section.

Learning activity

- Recapping the verses, choruses and middle (QCA unit 15:1).
- Recapping rap section from the previous lesson (QCA unit 15:7).
- Writing their own rap (QCA units 19:1 and 21:6).
- Deciding on appropriate movements (QCA unit 15:8).

QCA learning objectives

Unit 15 Ongoing skills

'This unit highlights the musical skills that require regular practice and ongoing development throughout the key stage.'
'Singing songs with control and using the voice expressively.'

- Section 1 – Children should learn about breathing, dynamics and accuracy of pitch.

'Listening, memory and movement.'
Children should learn:

- Section 7 – to listen with sustained concentration; to remember longer pieces of music; about metre.
- Section 8 – to respond physically to music with understanding of musical features.

Unit 19 Songwriter – Exploring lyrics and melody

'This unit develops children's ability to compose a song with an awareness of the relationship between lyrics and melody.'
'How does a song use lyrics?'

- Section 1 – Children should learn what is meant by the term 'lyrics' and how they can reflect the time and place in which they were written.

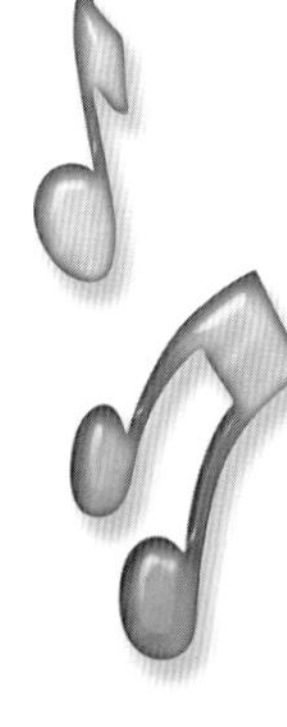

Unit 21 Exploring musical processes

'This unit provides an opportunity for children to develop and demonstrate the musical skills, knowledge and understanding achieved in Years 5 and 6.'
'Composing music to a specific brief.'

- Section 6 – Children should learn to use different starting points to create a composition.

Scottish attainment targets

Expressing feelings, ideas, thought and solutions (creating and designing)

- Level D – Invent music which incorporates simple melodic and rhythmic features and shows imagination and some awareness of structures.

Lesson 4 The rap

1 Lead the class in a class warm-up. Form a circle and place hands on heads and make the siren sounds. Next repeat the 'Tarzan' cry, drumming the upper chest gently with fists. Finally, after the count of 3, have everyone stamp forward and shout 'HA', pulling their elbows as they stamp. Repeat with 'HO' and 'HEE'.

2 Play the song through on TRACK 26 and sing along together.

3 Now play the rap section on TRACK 36 and have everyone rap along.

4 Ask the children to suggest words or phrases related to the theme of the song and write these up on the whiteboard – scribble all over the board, but try to arrange them roughly in groups of similar rhyming words. Try to leave the ideas shouted out in the exact wording that the children express.

5 Using this 'rhyme board', encourage the children to try to come up with four more lines for the rap – see if they can find meaningful phrases using the rhyme word at the end of each line. This way children will associate words and feelings and most importantly their own expression.

6 Now try the completed rap section, playing TRACK 36, and add your new section at the end. If the children have trouble writing the new lines, leave it out and continue the lesson.

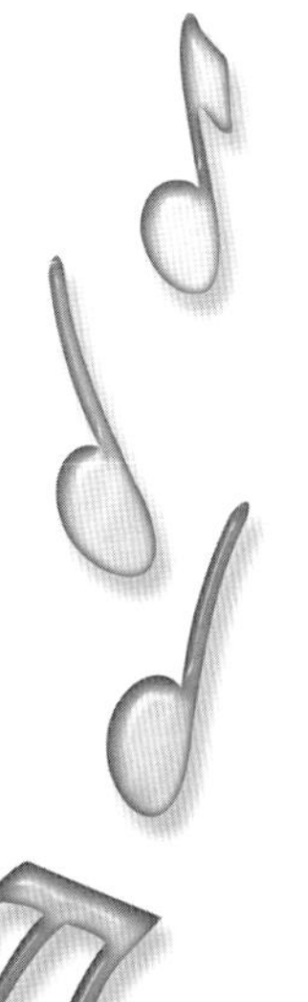

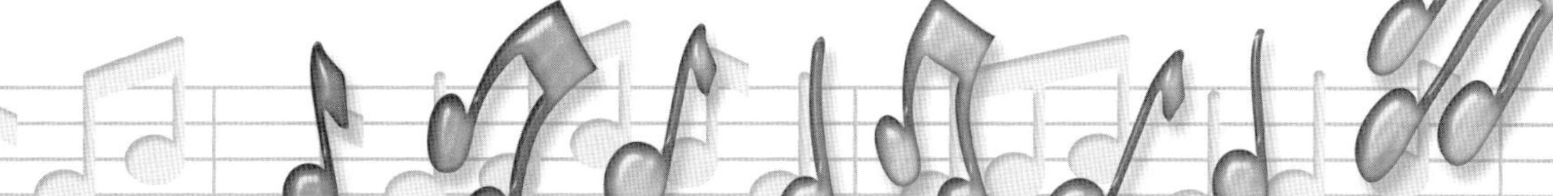

The rap

7 Next, collect all the percussion instruments and recap the pulse and rhythm arrangement on TRACKS 31 and 32.

8 Play, sing and rap through the song, using TRACK 26, then go through the whole song again but this time using TRACK 27 (the backing track) to see whether the children can manage without the supporting voice.

9 Explain to the children that it adds variety to a performance to use smaller groups for some sections. Choose small groups of six or seven children to have a go at the rap section on their own (you can use the pulse on TRACK 31 as backing). Give a number of small groups a go, and ask the children who was most serious when they were rapping.

Chill out time!

Have the children sit down at their desks. Each child should lay their head on their arms with eyes closed, breathing slowly through their nose. Encourage them to stay silent and listen to the sounds around them for two minutes. Ask them to think about their favourite school dinner, to remember how they travelled to school that morning, to think about what it would be like if they had to run four miles to school every day or if there was no school dinner – would they be too tired to learn anything? Once the children have had time to think, have them sit up and then go around the class asking them to share their thoughts.

Lesson 5 Moods and feelings

Note – You will be using the instrument trolley for this lesson.

Music objective

Exploring musical processes.

Learning activity

- Composing music using a range of different sounds and musical ideas in response to a task set by Music Works (QCA unit 21:1).
- Recapping song (QCA unit 15:7).
- Recapping percussion parts (QCA unit 15:7).

QCA learning objectives

Unit 15 Ongoing skills

'This unit highlights the musical skills that require regular practice and ongoing development throughout the key stage.'
'Listening, memory and movement.'

- Section 7 – Children should learn to listen with sustained concentration; to remember longer pieces of music; about metre.

Unit 21 Exploring musical processes

'This unit provides an opportunity for children to develop and demonstrate the musical skills, knowledge and understanding achieved in Years 5 and 6.'
'How do composers begin to compose?'

- Section 1 – Children should learn how music is composed from a variety of different stimuli.

Scottish attainment targets

Expressing feelings, ideas, thought and solutions (creating and designing)

- Level D – Invent music which incorporates simple melodic and rhythmic features and shows imagination and some awareness of structures and contrasts; represent inventions visually in a simplified form of notation.

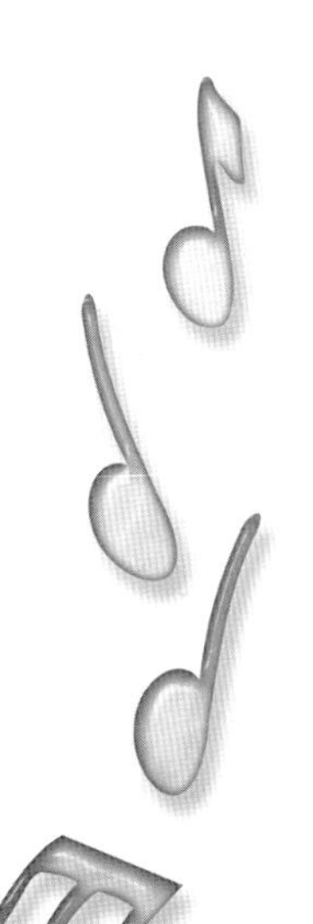

World poverty

Lesson 5 Moods and feelings

1 Lead the children in a warm-up as in Lesson 1. Invite the children to add something to the warm-up if they would like.

2 In this lesson, we leave the song temporarily and explore music in another way. Ask the children to sit in a circle and remain quiet. Tell them they are going to listen to three pieces of music and will have to answer questions on it.

3 Play TRACKS 33, 34 and 35 on the CD and listen to three musical sections. Ask the children which one describes Africa, which Australia and which America.

4 Having established that, split the class in to three groups and give out musical instruments.

5 Ask each group to create a short musical piece based on one of the three countries; don't tell the other groups which one they decide to interpret. Spend time with each group and encourage them to try different instruments.

6 Have each group perform their short piece to the other groups and ask the others to guess which country is being portrayed.

7 Return to the song – play TRACK 32 and recap the rhythm parts to the song.

8 Play TRACK 26 and sing and rap along together. Ask the children to play percussion at the relevant section. Remember to include movements selected for the rap part and ask all those not rapping in that section to bob down on one knee, in order to give a dynamic to the visual performance. Once the rap part is over, they can quickly stand and sing as soon as the chorus comes in.

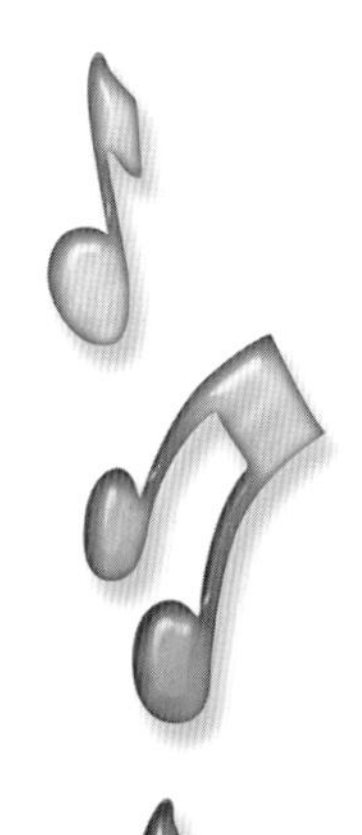

Lesson 5 Moods and feelings

9 Practise the song again with TRACK 26, then run through using TRACK 27 (the backing track). Choose a small group to perform the rap on their own, reminding the other children to come in strongly after the rap to keep the energy going.

10 See if there are any children who would like to perform the song up to the end of the rap in a small group for the rest of the class. Encourage the other children to give them lots of applause at the end.

Chill out time!

Have the children lie down and relax on the floor, closing their eyes and breathing slowly. Try to induce total silence. Ask the children to listen to the sounds around them. After a suitable amount of time, ask the children to sit up again, then go round the class one by one, asking each child to recount the different sounds they heard. Answers might include: the sound of someone breathing; the distant sound of cars or traffic; birds outside; voices from the classroom next door; someone in the room giggling.

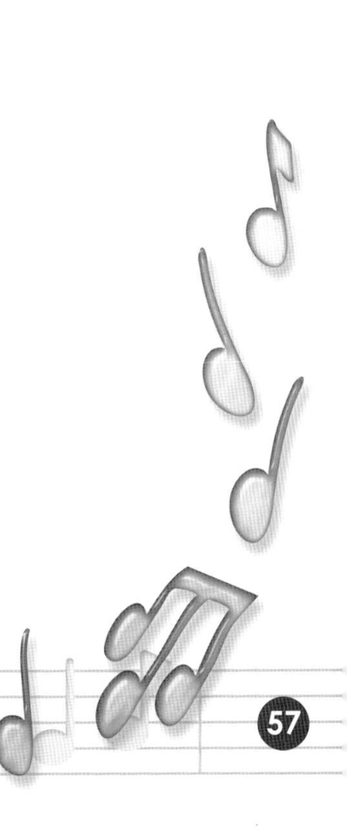

Lesson 6 The performance

Music objective

Developing the ability to take part in a class performance with confidence, expression and control.

Learning activity

- Performing together (QCA units 15:1, 15:7 and 20:1).
- Doing a vocal warm-up (QCA unit 15:1).

QCA learning objectives

Unit 15 Ongoing skills

'This unit highlights the musical skills that require regular practice and ongoing development throughout the key stage.'

'Singing songs with control and using the voice expressively.'

- Section 1 – Children should learn about breathing, dynamics and accuracy of pitch.

'Listening, memory and movement.'

- Section 7 – Children should learn to listen with sustained concentration; to remember longer pieces of music; about metre.

Unit 20 Stars, hide your fires – performing together

'This unit develops and demonstrates children›s ability to take part in a class performance with confidence, expression and control.'

'What is the song about?'

- Section 1 – Children should learn about the context of the song selected.

Scottish attainment targets

Expressing feelings, ideas, thought and solutions (communicating and presenting)

- Levels A–E – When and where appropriate, present and perform music to the teacher, another group, the rest of the class or a wider audience.

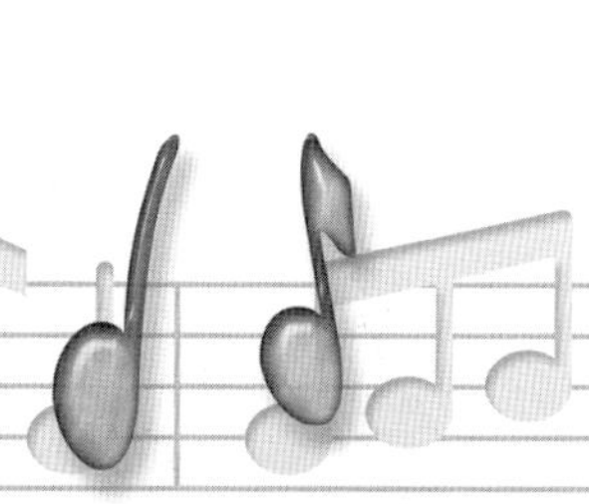
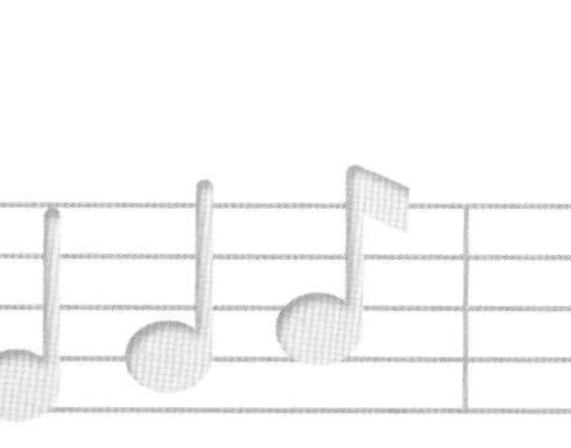

Lesson 6 The performance

1 Performance can be limited to the classroom. It can be later performed at a school assembly or included in a school play. You will need to use TRACK 27 (the backing track) for the performance.

2 Guide the children through a warm-up, as in Lesson 1.

3 Practise the rap part first, using TRACK 36 on the CD.

4 Run through the choruses and harmonies using TRACK 29.

5 Prepare all the percussion instruments and run through the percussion parts, playing TRACK 32 if necessary.

6 Arrange the children into their performing positions, perhaps in a 'choir' formation in two rows.

7 Have the children perform the song as well as possible. Children often do their best rendition the first time through, so if you are going to get the children to perform in front of others, try not to let them sing it all the way through, just refresh sections beforehand. Ask the children if there are any parts they find difficult and rehearse these.

8 For fun, let half the class perform to the other half and then swap over, or boys to girls then girls to boys. The half listening are allowed to pull faces and try to 'put off' the performers but they must not make a sound. This leads to stifled laughter and a great deal of fun. Explain to the children the reason for this is so they may get used to performing in front of people without being 'put off'. It can lead to a strengthening in concentration.

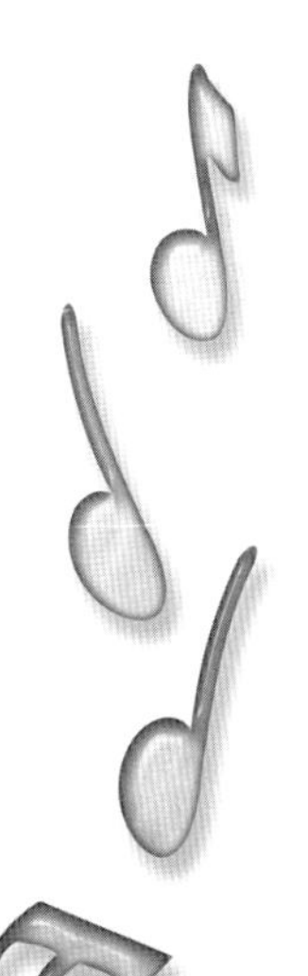

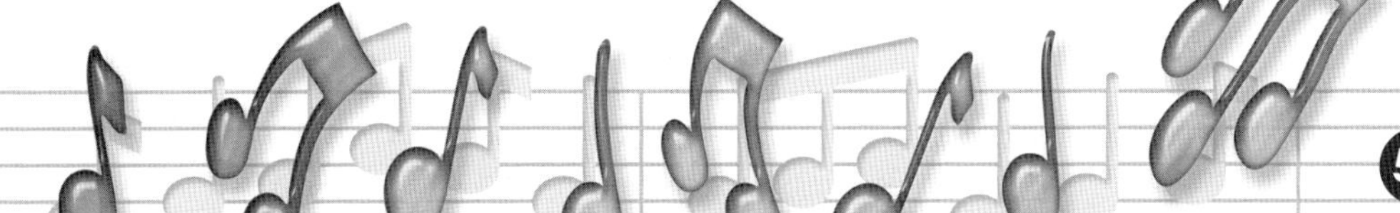

The performance

9 Decide with the children how they are going to end the song – for example, perhaps they are going to get quieter over the last two or three lines. Then play TRACK 27 and have the children perform their version over the backing track.

10 If there is an opportunity to do so, take the children along with the CD player into the hall and let them try performing the song in a different setting, to let them get used to a place other than the classroom. Make sure they feel relaxed and that it's not a performance in front of others at this stage.

Have the children lie on the floor and relax. Ask them to think about what their favourite part of the song is and if they were to write a song, what it would be.

This Friend of Mine

Chorus
Oh let me tell you about him,
This friend of mine.
He lives a long way away,
This friend of mine.
Oh let me tell you about him,
This friend of mine.
He lives a long way away.
This friend of mine.

Verse
He ain't got no shoes,
He ain't got no money,
He ain't got no school,
He ain't got no mummy.

Chorus
Oh let me tell you about him,
This friend of mine.
He lives a long way away,
This friend of mine.
Oh let me tell you about him,
This friend of mine.
He lives a long way away.
This friend of mine.

Verse
I remember him laughing
And we would play all day, all day.
Now I can hear him crying
Coz he's too weak to play, today.

Rap
Coz now his hunger's
Forced him under.
Ain't got no home,
He's got to wander.
He's had to walk for days and days
In search of water, in search of bread.
There's no one left to care for him,
Everyone he loves is dead.
There's no one left to care for him,
Everyone he loves is dead.

Chorus
Oh let me tell you about him,
This friend of mine.
He lives a long way away,
This friend of mine.
Oh let me tell you about him,
This friend of mine.
He lives a long way away.
This friend of mine.

Rap gap

Chorus
Oh let me tell you about him,
This friend of mine,
He lives a long way away,
This friend of mine.
Oh let me tell you about him,
This friend of mine,
He lives a long way away,
This friend of mine.

GOOD LUCK WITH YOUR PERFORMANCE!
(Note: This performance can take place in the classroom, in front of the whole school at assembly, or as part of a school play. Wherever you perform it, make sure you all have fun doing it!)

FOLLOW YOUR HEART
DONALDSON&McCOURT
♩ = 100
YOU'VE GOT TO FOL - LOW YOUR HEART FOL - LOW YOUR HEART
HOPE IT MEANS YOU'VE GOT THE COU - RAGE TO FOL - LOW YOUR DREAMS HOPE AND PRAY THAT
LIGHT WILL GUIDE YOUR WAY YOU'VE GOT TO FOL - LOW YOUR HEART FOL - LOW YOUR HEART
FOL - LOW YOUR HEART OH YEAH YOU'VE GOT TO
FINE
24
RAP SECTION
HAVE YOUR DREAMS AND
FAS - CI - NA - TION MAKE YOUR DREAMS A RE - AL - I - SA - TION BUT IN THIS WORLD YOU DON'T
GET A FREE MEAL YOU'VE GOT TO WORK HARD TO MAKE IT REAL
D.S. AL FINE

♩=135
FAMILY TREE
MCCOURT&DONALDSON
INTRO
C G F G
WHY IN THE WORLD ARE WE FIGHT - ING ON END - LESS - LY
PI - CKING ON ONE ANO - THER THEY'RE NOT THE SAME AS ME
BIRDS THAT ARE IN THE TREES DIFF - ER - ENT FEATH - ERS AND BREEDS
HU - MMING BIRDS SOFT AND GEN - TLE WHILE THE EA - GLE IS PROUD AND FREE
WE ALL LIVE AND BREATHE OUR CO - LOUR AND OUR CRE - ED DON'T
MA - TTER MUCH TO ME WE'RE ALL FROM THE SAME ALL FROM THE SAME
EMI7 AMI7 FMAJ7
F/G
REPEAT 2ND TIME
RAP SECTION 16
ALL FROM THE SAME FAM'-LY TREE
WHY IN THE WORLD CAN'T WE LIVE AS ONE FA - MI - LY
SO MA - NY BRAN - CHES ON JUST ONE TREE THERE'S ROOM FOR US ALL TO GROW
END - LESS - LY
D.S. AL FINE

FRIEND OF MINE
McCOURT&DONALDSON
INTRO
OH LET ME TELL YOU A- BOUT__ HIM__ THIS FRIEND OF MINE__ HE LIVES A LONG WAY A- WAY
THIS FRIEND OF MINE__ OH LET ME TELL YOU A- BOUT__ HIM__ THIS FRIEND OF MINE
HE LIVES A LONG WAY A- WAY___ THIS FRIEND OF MINE__
HE AIN'T GOT__ NO__ SHOES HE AIN'T GOT__ NO__ MO - NEY__
HE AIN'T GOT__ NO__ SCHOOL HE AIN'T GOT__ NO__ MU- MMY___
OH LET ME TELL YOU A- BOUT__ HIM__ THIS FRIEND OF MINE
HE LIVES A LONG WAY A- WAY___ THIS FRIEND OF MINE__ OH LET ME TELL YOU A BOUT
HIM__ THIS FRIEND OF MINE__ HE LIVES A LONG WAY A- WAY___ THIS FRIEND OF MINE
I RE - MEM - BER HIM LAUGH - ING__

AND WE WOULD PLAY ALL DAY ALL DAY__ NOW I CAN HEAR HIM CRY - ING__
'COS HE'S TOO WEAK TO PLAY TO- DAY___
RAP SECTION
OH LET ME TELL YOU A- BOUT HIM__ THIS FRIEND OF MINE
HE LIVES A LONG WAY A- WAY___ THIS FRIEND OF MINE__ OH LET ME TELL YOU A- BOUT
HIM__ THIS FRIEND OF MINE__ HE LIVES A LONG WAY A- WAY___ THIS FRIEND OF MINE
OH LET ME TELL YOU A- BOUT__ HIM__ THIS FRIEND OF MINE
HE LIVES A LONG WAY A- WAY___ THIS FRIEND OF MINE__ OH LET ME TELL YOU A- BOUT
HIM__ THIS FRIEND OF MINE__ HE LIVES A LONG WAY A- WAY__
THIS FRIEND OF MINE__ ROAH!

Self advocacy

Look carefully at the CD covers and packages your teacher has brought in. Design a cover for your favourite song or artist. If you don't have one, you could design a cover for a compilation called *Moments of Mine* – or perhaps your teacher can suggest a different title for you to use.

Family tree – differences and inclusion

Ask your parents about the songs and rhymes they sang when they were at school. Can they teach them to you? Perhaps you could record them singing instead. Ask them about why they sang the songs – perhaps they were for celebrations such as weddings or birthday parties, for worship, to help them learn their times tables, for when they were running or playing games, or to voice a protest against something. Perform the song for your class (or play your recording) and tell them about it.

World poverty

Your teacher will bring in pictures to do with the song or its country of origin and show you how to make them into jigsaw puzzles. Make a puzzle out of your picture and then share it with your friends.

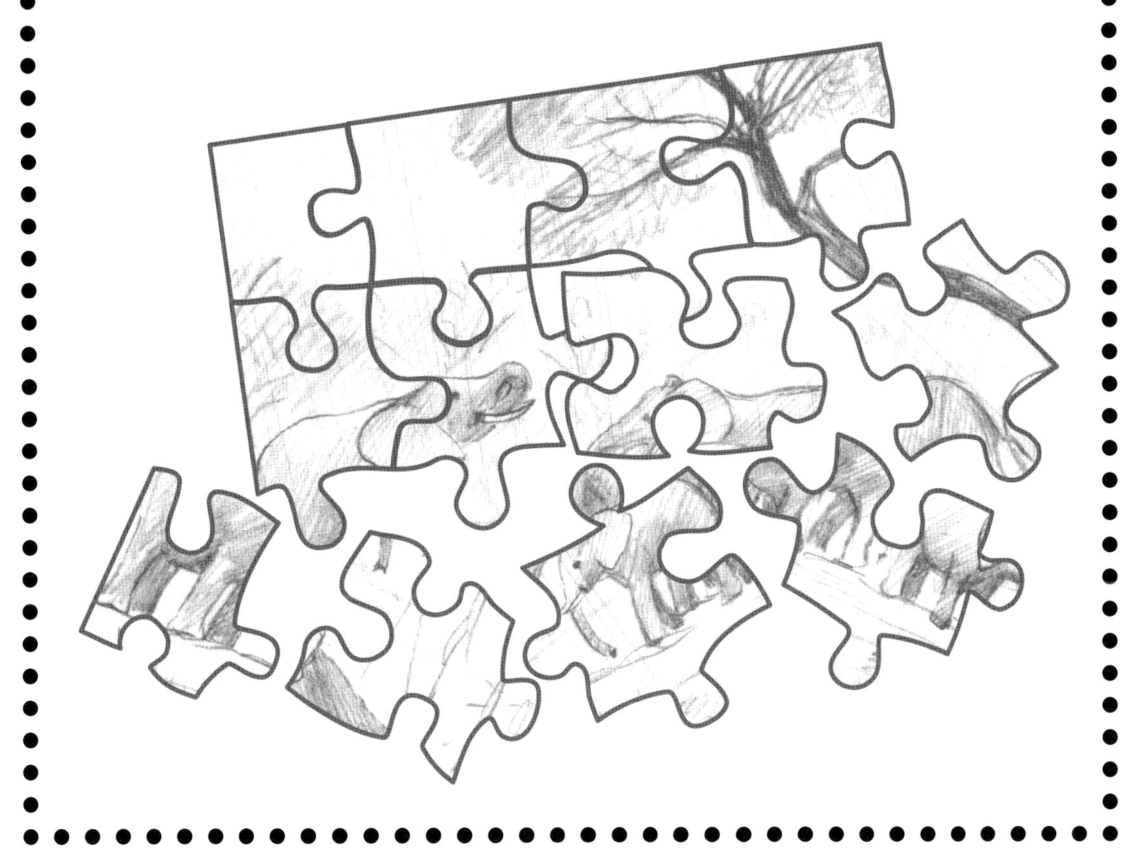

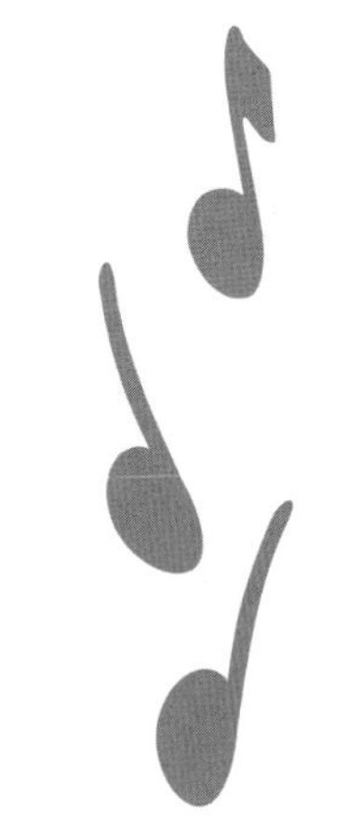

In lots of places around the world people make instruments out of 'found' objects. See what musical instruments you could make – perhaps you could use an old tin to make a drum, or a shaker using rice or pasta shells. Experiment with the different sounds you can get from other types of material – egg whisks, bin lids, wrapping paper, bubble wrap, corrugated card... What other things can you think of?